HISTORY FILES　　Voyages of Discovery

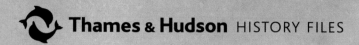
Thames & Hudson HISTORY FILES

Voyages of Discovery

DAVID BOYLE

HALF TITLE Late 15th-century Portuguese silver plate depicting a caravel.
TITLE PAGES Captain Cook arrives in Huahine in French Polynesia, 1769.
BELOW A 16th-century depiction of a Portuguese encounter in India.

First published in 2011 in paperback in the United States of America by
Thames & Hudson Inc., 500 Fifth Avenue, New York, New York 10110

thamesandhudsonusa.com

Library of Congress Catalog Card Number 2011922605

ISBN 978-0-500-28959-4

Printed in China through Asia Pacific Offset Ltd

Contents

Introduction: Maps, Motivation and Meetings

In the 1960s the Canadian journalist Dorothy Harley Eber began to travel to the Arctic north, armed with a tape recorder. She continued to visit for the next four decades, collecting the stories that had been passed down from generation to generation by the Inuit. What she and other oral historians found was not only a wealth of material stretching as far back as the first English expeditions to the area under Martin Frobisher, 400 years previously, but also – hidden in the memory bank – a glimpse of one of those extraordinary encounters between explorers and explored. Transported back well over a century, they listened to the tale of the first encounter between the Inuit and the men of Sir John Franklin's doomed expedition of the 1840s: lost in the ice, their skin black, their upper lips frozen off, their eyes gaunt, the newcomers looked more like walking spirits than men.[1]

Franklin's own portrait of an Inuit and his son, whom he met in the Arctic on an expedition in the 1820s.

OPPOSITE HMS *Resolute* is abandoned in the Arctic ice in May 1854, after the failure of a search for Franklin's missing ships and crews.

The precise fate of Franklin and his two ships, the *Erebus* and the *Terror*, has always been mysterious. As with so many of the European pioneers, the details of their encounters with those who inhabited the newly discovered lands have been largely airbrushed out of history. But as she listened to the Inuit account Eber uncovered memories not just of the ghostly figures of Franklin's crews, dressed so inadequately for the Arctic, but also of the Inuit, helping them with food and maps.

This vision of the past is so striking not only because it reveals the hidden history of exploration, but also because it is very rare. There are other interviews, often given by old people who could

Dog-faced men were among the legendary creatures that medieval explorers expected to meet in far-flung lands.

remember James Cook's arrival in Australia in their distant youth, but otherwise very little exists. The rest of what we know about the first meetings between civilizations has been mediated through the memories and histories of the explorers, rather than the explored. These accounts go right back to Christopher Columbus, and even earlier.

So where does one start? Encounters between cultures have always taken place, a long time before Columbus first presented his proposal to search for a western route to Asia to Queen Isabella of Castile. Our natural inquisitiveness has forever led humankind to explore – and to cross – the limits of the known world. The Polynesians probably colonized New Zealand only one thousand years ago. The Vikings managed to use the sun and the Pole Star to steer to Newfoundland, Kiev, Antioch and (travelling partly by land) to the Caspian Sea. They may have even reached the Far East. Some journeys are legendary, such as the tale of St Brendan, who met a whale as he sailed a glorified coracle westwards from Ireland (though even the accounts of Brendan's voyage have the ring of authenticity in parts).

Some are on the fringes of history, such as the Phoenician circum-navigation of Africa in 600 BC described by Herodotus. Others are backed up by clear evidence, like the twelve-year journey of the Chinese ambassador who set out in 139 BC and reached as far as the Hellenized kingdom of Bactria.

Goods often travelled further than people. The Romans had trade links stretching to the Indian Ocean; and Marco Polo revealed to a European public the full extent of the Silk Road. They generally discounted him as a fraud, but they had been receiving silks and spices for generations, passed from trader to trade along the route. When John Cabot made his way to Mecca in order to discover the origin of the spices that his compatriots craved, he found that nobody knew: through an intricate network of traders, the precious cargo had travelled one third of the way around the world.

Trade, then, was the principal reason for cross-cultural encounters. By the 15th century the Indian Ocean and the Mediterranean were emerging as the hubs of commerce, as the appetite for the world's luxuries began to grow. But trade was not the only incitement for travel: 'One motive is fame, another curiosity, and a third is lust

Merchants from India arriving in Ormuz, the powerful trading centre for the Persian Gulf and Indian Ocean in the 13th and 14th centuries.

for gain,' a chronicler explained in 1240, struggling to understand why people went to Greenland.[2] Fame was certainly important; and those who followed the mysterious half-English, half-Portuguese prince known as Henry the Navigator were motivated by a culture of chivalric adventure that had emerged in the early 15th century.

Another motivation was religion. Starting with St Paul, Christianity drove followers of the new faith across the seas. Islam, on the other hand, brought pilgrims to Mecca and forged new links between the Mediterranean and the Indian and Persian worlds. By the 7th century AD, there were Muslim ships at the mouth of the Indus, and Arabs were meeting Chinese traders on the Malay peninsula. Mecca, too, became one of those key places where different worlds intersected, where people came together in great numbers to

A 13th-century caravan, loaded down with merchandise and bound for Mecca – one of those key points on the globe where different cultures met and traded.

trade, and where cultural differences were put aside in the common pursuit of wealth. Indeed, in English the city's name is used to mean a place of great attraction.

There is no doubt that the Chinese were at the centre of many such networks. Looked at objectively, they should have been the ones to make the great breakthrough of recognizing the shape of the globe. The Yongle Emperor seized the throne in 1402 and sent more than seventy missions from China over the next two decades, demanding 'tribute'. Between 1405 and 1433, there were seven expeditions by sea under the leadership of Admiral Zheng He. The first of these comprised 62 junks and 225 support ships; some of the biggest of these may have been over 3,000 tons. There are records of medieval ships in the Mediterranean weighing 1,000 tons, but the average size

ABOVE One of the navigational diagrams drawn during Zheng He's expeditions in the early Ming dynasty, this one giving directions from Sri Lanka to Sumatra.

Admiral Zheng He brought a giraffe back to China, a gift for the emperor from the Sultan of Malindi in East Africa.

A copy of the vast Ebstorf mappa mundi (the original map was destroyed in World War II). The original map, some 3.6 m (12 ft) square, was created in the second half of the 13th century. It shows Christ – his head at the top, his hands at the sides, and his feet at the bottom – gathering up the world.

was closer to just one tenth of this. When he returned from his fourth voyage – at roughly the time when the battle of Agincourt was fought in Europe – Zheng He brought back a giraffe. Seven years later, in 1421, he may have set out along the west coast of Africa, reaching Mombasa and Zanzibar.

What would European history have been like if one of those huge junks had loomed out of the mist and put in at Lisbon or Bristol? We will never know, but the fact remains that the Chinese (and others) had better navigation technology than anyone in Western Europe at the time. Yet once the Confucian elite in China had clawed its way back to power in the 1420s, and the threat from Mongolia increased, they ended the voyages and destroyed most of the records.

In the event, circumstances, technology and philosophy all conspired so that, in the 1490s, the basic outline of the main continents suddenly became known to the Europeans. It was a critical breakthrough. From this point on there was an extraordinary explosion in exploration. Within the next three centuries, the world was mapped, parcelled up, looted and re-imagined.

By far the biggest breakthroughs in understanding the globe's geography came in little more than thirty years, between the time of Columbus's first Atlantic voyage, in 1492, to Magellan's circumnavigation of the globe twenty-seven years later. Why was this period so fruitful in terms of exploration? It was partly because the western frontiers of Europe had been shrinking as winter temperatures dipped, freezing the descendants of the Vikings out of their Greenland settlements. It was partly that the techniques of navigation, knowledge of Atlantic currents and the development of caravels, rigged to sail much closer to the wind, all came together at the same time in Europe. But there was also a new philosophical spirit abroad. Exploration was a business proposition for pioneers such as Columbus, John Cabot and their rivals, who were driven by the closure of the East to European traders following the fall of Constantinople to the Turks in 1453. Yet at the same time their ventures were informed by Renaissance knowledge and ideology. Both Columbus and Cabot, and Amerigo Vespucci too, had personal links to the so-called Sage of Florence, Paolo dal Pozzo Toscanelli, who first proposed that one could reach the East by sailing west.

Equally, no westward voyage of this kind would have been attempted had Toscanelli and his followers not seriously underestimated the size of the earth – the result of a combination of hubris and flawed mathematics that emerged from the Renaissance as surely as Michelangelo and Leonardo da Vinci, who were part of the same generation.

By the time Columbus died, in May 1506, the existence of the Americas was well known (though Columbus himself never accepted it). The problems that faced the next generation were both political

Martin Behaim's globe, the earliest surviving of its kind. It was made in 1492, the year that Columbus first set out for the Indies, and so does not show the Americas.

and geographical: political because of the Pope's arbitrary division of the world into Portuguese and Spanish; geographical because there had to be – or so the pioneers believed – a sea route through the new continent. But whether that was a Northwest Passage, a Southwest Passage or a more convenient gap in Central America, nobody knew.

These voyages, and those like them, chipped away at the remaining geographical ignorance of the human race, creating ever more opportunities for meetings between previously alien cultures. In 1689, for example, two centuries after Columbus, there were negotiations between the Russians and Chinese at the Amur River (which still forms much of the modern border between Russia and China). The talks were conducted in Latin because the Chinese envoys were accompanied by two European missionaries, and the Russian delegation included a Roman Catholic from Poland. It was a key moment in the march of globalization.

But all this also multiplied the opportunities for misunderstanding. When the Portuguese reached Canton (now Guangzhou) on the southeast Chinese coast in 1517, they outraged the locals by firing a cannon in salute. Later, it became well known among Chinese colonies that the Portuguese ate small children, with published descriptions of how they boiled and roasted them. There were continuing misunderstandings about the gifts that each side gave the other,

The 1502 map made by Alberto Cantino, a secret agent at the Portuguese court, and smuggled out of Portugal to show the extent of their discoveries. The vertical line in the Atlantic divides the world into two spheres of influence: Spanish to the west and Portuguese to the east.

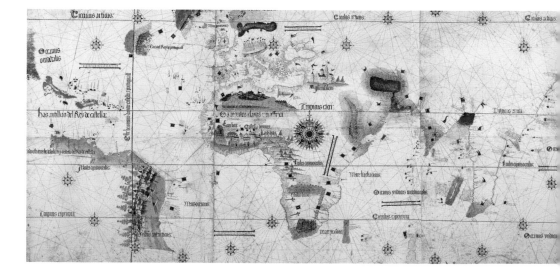

Earl Macartney, leader of the first British embassy to China, meets the Chinese emperor. This watercolour was painted by William Alexander, who accompanied the mission.

whether they were the glass beads with which Columbus greeted the people of the New World or the gold, spices or furs that were passed the other way. In the Arctic, the Inuit gave furs without expecting anything in return, but rather as part of a ritual of meeting and welcome. The metal kettles they received were often cut up instead of being used for their intended purpose. Gifts seem to have had a symbolic value for the indigenous populations, not an economic one. Once they realized that the new arrivals were not supernatural beings from another world, the evidence is that they lost interest in their trinkets. The misunderstandings about gifts persisted in China, whose diplomats saw any present as 'tribute'. The British Macartney mission to Beijing in 1793 brought a huge array of presents for the Chinese emperor at the time, who frustrated Earl Macartney by commending King George III for his respectful spirit of submission.[3]

What made it possible to communicate at all in these first meetings was partly the common humanity of those involved. Columbus believed he recognized the hand signals given by the Indians he encountered. Magellan ordered his men to copy the dance of welcome given by the 'giants' they met in Patagonia to put them at their ease (although this didn't stop him seizing one of them). But far

This gold telescope, adorned with enamel and pearls, was presented by Earl Macartney to the Chinese emperor in 1793.

more important than this were the roles of intermediaries, most of them forgotten by formal history.

Since the early 1440s, Portuguese explorers had been seizing inhabitants of new places, taking them back to Portugal and teaching them the language, while leaving behind members of the crew to learn the local language and win round the people they were staying with. Magellan knew he had finally made it around the world when his slave interpreter was able to make himself understood in Malay. A group of Taíno people from the Bahamas were brought back to Spain after Columbus's first Atlantic crossing; they were taught Spanish by Vespucci in Seville.

Even with the presence of intermediaries, the encounters were always fraught with dangerous moments of distrust, and often degenerated into violence. Sometimes they left burned villages and slaughtered villagers, sometimes whole civilizations were destroyed. Occasionally it was the explorers themselves who suffered. Both Magellan and Cook died at the hands of the people they encountered. But the risk was usually the other way. Over and over again, the gift-giving of the first encounter turned suddenly into slaughter, partly because of the sheer firepower of the Europeans. They overwhelmed the cultures they encountered because they were that much more prepared to be brutal, and had the technology to be so.

There was often confusion among the newly discovered people about where the explorers came from. When English explorer John Smith's men captured a Native American called Amoroleck by the Rappahannock River in 1608, they asked him why his hunting party had attacked them. He said that he had heard they 'were a people come from under the world, to take their world from them.'[4] Somewhat controversial accounts of the first encounter in Manhattan suggest that the locals believed the approaching ship was a giant fish; as it got closer, they believed it was a large house carrying God. Columbus described an old man coming on board who said: 'Come, see the people who have come from the sky; bring them something to eat and drink.'[5] For those people who had never encountered Europeans before, the overwhelming feeling may have been that they were having a supernatural experience.

But it is harder to be sure what either side meant by 'supernatural'. Even the peoples Vasco da Gama encountered in India had few written records, and most of their oral traditions and cultures were destroyed by what followed. The conquistador Hernando de Soto found towns in America already grassed over in the 1540s because so many of the locals had died from diseases brought by the invaders. There are 18th-century descriptions of woods full of the bodies of Native Americans who had succumbed to smallpox.[6] Those who died took the knowledge of their encounters with them.

The pattern of encounters: this was the 'defensive' action in 1616 by the Dutch Le Maire and Schouten expedition at the Hoorn Islands; it was followed by a fortnight of trading and mutual entertainment.

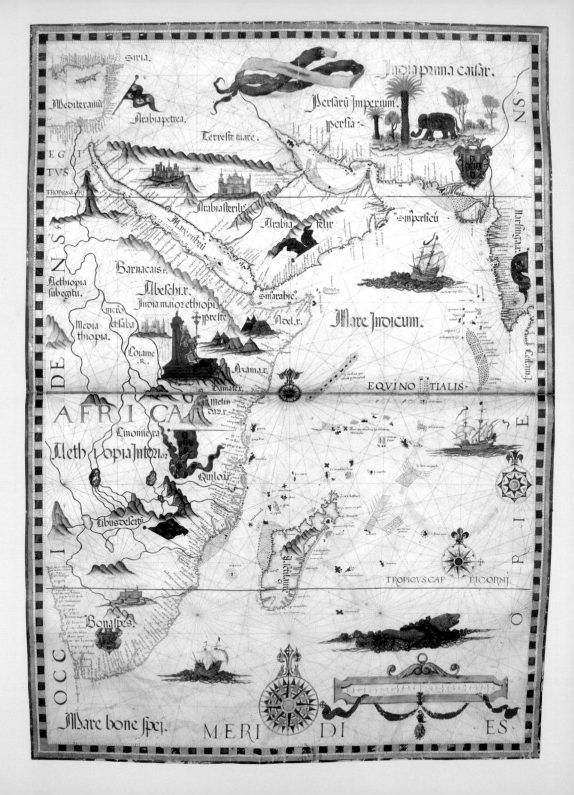

Chapter 1

The Sea Route to India: Dias and da Gama

The early Renaissance in 15th-century Europe was a romantic period. The age of chivalry was dead in practice, but the emerging generations of young aristocrats and artists were fascinated by history, and by the idea of chivalry, of Arthurian adventure and chivalric prowess. They also dreamed of, among other mysteries, the legendary Christian king, Prester John, who it was thought would one day exercise his huge wealth and power to rescue Europe from the perceived Muslim threat. The romance of Prester John was as potent as that of King Arthur, with the added excitement that Prester John was supposed to be living.

Among those obsessed with the idea of finding him was a former pirate and holder of the monopoly of the Portuguese soap trade, Prince Henry, known to history as 'the Navigator'. Henry had dreamed up a plan to sail around Africa to reach the Indies and Cipangu, Marco Polo's name for Japan. There was little evidence that such a voyage was possible, except for the legend of Hannibal sailing all the way round Africa in the same direction. In fact, many geographers believed that Africa went all the way down to the South Pole.

But with promises of glory, Henry's emissaries tracked down the greatest shipwrights, mathematicians, astronomers and geographers and lured them to his new institute for navigation and geography at Sagres in the far southwest of Portugal. This windswept edge of the known world, the last rocky outcrop at the most southwesterly point of Europe, gave an aura of sanctity to the whole enterprise. Under Henry's leadership, Portuguese expeditions sailed

Prince Henry 'the Navigator', the half-English obsessive who used his soap-trading monopoly to finance an extraordinary series of expeditions.

OPPOSITE Prester John sits on a throne in the heart of East Africa in this mid-16th-century map, which also shows some of the Portuguese discoveries by Vasco da Gama and those who came after him.

African encounters: this is the 17th-century servant of Don Miguel de Castro, brought back to Europe from West Africa.

to discover whether the sea was really boiling at the equator or if the pitch which held the boats together would melt there. Henry was the godfather of European exploration and the instigator of a tradition of encounters with other peoples, and other worlds, which set a pattern recognizable for centuries. It was Henry whose captains first used the technique of seizure; their journeys needed guides, so they captured passing strangers and somehow educated, terrified or cajoled them into learning enough to be useful.

The first Africans were seized in this way in 1441 by the young Antão Gonçalves, Henry the Navigator's chamberlain. He had been sent to Rio de Ouro in Western Sahara to get skins and oil, and was ordered – like the others – to go further into the unknown. The river had been named as such (River of Gold) by Portuguese navigator and explorer Gil Eannes in 1435, the first to round Cape Bojador, a headland on the northern coast of what is now Western Sahara (he found footprints and camels, but no people). It was Gonçalves's idea that a captive would be of assistance. He and a team landed after dark, marched until they found a path and some footprints, and caught one naked man, and a woman on the way back. It was an ominously significant moment: the first of millions of Africans who would eventually be forced into slavery by the Europeans.

But great was the wonder of the people of the coast in seeing his caravel. ...Some thought it was a fish, others were sure it was a phantom, others again said it might be a bird that had that way of skimming along the surface of the sea.

Contemporary description of a Portuguese expedition to Cape Verde in 1445[1]

Gonçalves returned later with twenty men to pursue an armed band they had seen in the distance. They killed three and took ten prisoners. Many of these early encounters would also involve potential translators brought out on the expedition. In this case it was one of Henry's Moorish slaves, but, as happened so often, he wasn't able to understand what they said. One of the new captives was an African noble called Adahu. He was taken back to Portugal and – once communication had been established – he frequently asked if he could go home, promising six others in his place. Henry eventually agreed, dressed him in beautiful clothes and sent him home, hoping that the clothes might lead to a trading opportunity. They waited for him to come back, but Adahu was never seen again. Yet the incident led to more serious slaving expeditions up the Rio de Ouro.

Three years later the Portuguese encountered black Africans again, this time near Cape Verde. Tradition suggests that both sides immediately faced the problem of categorization that would continue to trouble their successors through the centuries. Was this new arrival, with its sails fluttering in the breeze, real or supernatural? Was it animal or human? Were these people pagans or heathens? Christian or Muslim? Potential traders or potential slaves?

Henry the Navigator died in 1460, the year after the famous conference in Florence where the Portuguese discoveries were set before Paolo dal Pozzo Toscanelli, who would live to inspire Columbus. He had not fulfilled his dream of reaching the Indies, but by then, the Portuguese voyages had stepped up a gear, thanks to a revolutionary new ship, known as a caravel, and because of further developments in navigation, including star charts and methods for measuring the height of the sun and stars in the sky. In 1482, a

A mariner's astrolabe, known in Europe from the late 15th century, shown being used to determine latitude from the noon altitude of the sun.

Medieval seafarers used to cling mainly to the coast, their square sail awkward in the wind if it failed to blow neatly from behind. The caravel was developed from Portuguese fishing boats under the direction of Henry the Navigator, possibly named after Arab boats called the *qarib*. Its triangular lateen sails allowed it to sail at sharper angles to the wind. The design not only made possible explorations down the African coast and out into the Atlantic, but it was also hugely influential because of the speed, manoeuvrability and economy of the ships. Two of Columbus's first small fleet, the *Niña* and *Pinta*, were caravels. The main disadvantage of the caravel was that it was generally too small for trading, rarely more than 160 tons. When Vasco da Gama made his famous voyage to India, he required something bigger – partly to carry goods and partly to survive the treacherous conditions around the Cape of Good Hope.

The development of the small and manoeuvrable caravel, influenced by the design of Arab boats, allowed the Portuguese to press on southwards along the African coast.

settlement and fort was developed at Elmina, on what is now the coast of Ghana, after negotiations with the local ruler Caramansa. Another pattern was emerging: the newcomers could be immensely strengthened by making alliances among the divided locals. It was a process which would eventually allow Cortés to conquer the Aztec civilization with just a few hundred men.

The Portuguese pioneers used to take wooden crosses to mark the coast at the limits of their investigations. The same year that Elmina was begun, Diogo Cão reached the mouth of the River Zaire, and began the tradition of pillars of white stone. Increasingly, the explorers were engaged in friendly relations with local rulers along the African coast, who particularly wanted the services of stonemasons and carpenters.

It was at this point that the superintendent of the Portuguese royal warehouses, a former pirate and slave-trader called Bartholomew Dias, was appointed to lead an expedition to go all the way around the tip of Africa and find a new trade route to India. He was also charged with finding the elusive Prester John. Dias sailed in August 1487, carrying with him two Africans seized by Cão and four women from the Guinea coast, dressed in finery and loaded down

BELOW The second of four stone markers, known as a padrão, left by Diogo Cão on the West African coast. It has the Portuguese royal shield on the front.

LEFT The Monument to the Discoveries, in Lisbon, showing a stone padrão being raised by the navigators Bartholomew Dias, Diogo Cão and António Abreu.

with samples of gold, silver and spices. These he took as far as he could inland, probably in the region of what is now the Gold Coast, in the hope that the news of them would reach Prester John.

The prevailing currents along the African coast south of the equator made it extremely hard simply to follow the coast down, so he took his small fleet of two ships plus a supply ship far out into the Atlantic, hoping to use more favourable winds and currents to swing out and back towards where he believed the tip of the continent might be. This technique had been developed by Portuguese navigators trying to find a way home after hugging the northern African coast southwards. It was how they had discovered the Azores and other Atlantic islands. Now Dias was attempting the same thing further south, gambling that the prevailing currents circulated the other way around in the southern hemisphere. Even for hardened mariners used to sticking close to the coast, these were frightening journeys into the unknown.

The 1489 world map by Henricus Martellus, showing the results of Portuguese exploration of the African coast, but created before Vasco da Gama's arrival in the Indian Ocean.

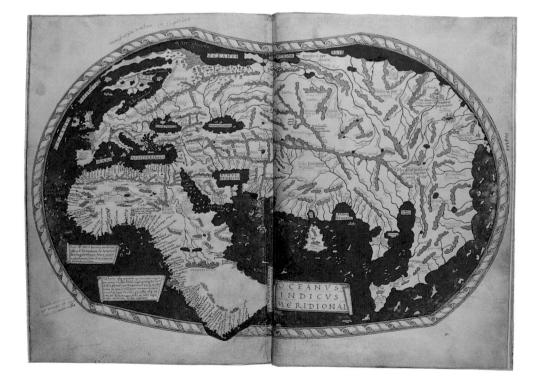

The route took Dias south, as planned, and then he struck off eastwards to look for the African coast. Nothing. So he turned north again, and there it was. The land continued to the east, so they must have rounded the tip of Africa. The first encounter took place in Mossel Bay, well east of the tip, but the locals were terrified at the apparition and drove their animals inland to safety. Dias carried on several hundred miles more to Cape Padrone and set up one of his white pillars. But he was about to run up against one of the main risks of explorers in the early days, which would cause problems for Columbus and Magellan and end the life of Henry Hudson: his crews dared not go further in case they wouldn't be able to return. Dias managed to agree that they would continue for two more days, but would turn back if the way to India did not then open out to the north. But it was not to be and, bitterly disappointed, he turned around. Finally finding the tip of Africa itself was a terrifying nautical ordeal, and he named it the Cape of Storms.

So it was an ambiguous homecoming to Lisbon, as Dias faced King John II and his advisors, among whom was Christopher Columbus, already hatching his own plans. On the plus side, Dias had proved that the Indian Ocean was not landlocked as the geographers had feared. There was, therefore, a sea route to the spice trade that bypassed the Muslim stranglehold over both the Black Sea and Arabia. There and then, John renamed the Cape of Storms the Cape of Good Hope. But the king was also furious that Dias had turned back so soon, instead of pressing on up the east coast of Africa.

It has never been quite clear why, but it was almost a decade before the next voyage around the Cape. Dias was asked to design and build ships weighty enough to withstand the storms, but John's unexpected death delayed matters. John had appointed the experienced royal servant Estêva da Gama in command, but he also died suddenly at around the same time as John, and the new King Manuel decided – after advice from his astrologers – that Estêva's son Vasco should take his place. Vasco heard the news when Manuel spotted him passing a doorway in the palace in Lisbon. Bartholomew Dias, the discoverer of the Cape of Good Hope, was overlooked because Manuel knew he needed a diplomat.

Vasco da Gama was then twenty-six, a discreet loner, in service to the noble Almeida family, and from a fishing village in the north of

JOÃO II

King John II, known as the 'Perfect Prince', was a ruthless enthusiast for exploration who breathed new life into the Portuguese African ventures.

Manuel I, the Portuguese king who ordered Vasco da Gama's first expedition to India, on the advice of his astrologer.

Portugal. His mother was partly English. Through early 1497, he struggled to get his fleet of galleons ready. He sailed in July and, in the Bay of St Helena on the southwest coast of Africa, faced one of those misunderstandings with the locals which were so common among explorers, and which was to have serious consequences.

Vasco's crew seized an African man, and brought him back to dine on the flagship *São Gabriel* at Gama's table. They let him go and the next day he came back with a number of others and, eventually, they managed to exchange some copper coins for conch shells. One of Vasco's men asked for permission to go back with the Africans. When he had eaten with them, his hosts indicated that it was time to go. But the boat sent to pick him up set out from the flagship too fast, and locals were unnerved. When it arrived, they flung their spears at it. Vasco and three others were slightly injured. The incident deepened the suspicion that the cautious Vasco had about local peoples of all kinds and it contributed to some of the bloodier incidents which were to come. Two days later, they sighted the Cape of Good Hope.

There were more contacts in southern and eastern Africa, and the kind of repeated misunderstandings that were to be so familiar. 'As soon as we saw them,' wrote Vasco's chronicler, 'we at once went ashore, and they began to play four or five flutes, and some played high and some played low, in a fashion that was very well attuned for blacks, of whom one does not expect music, and they danced like blacks. And the Captain-Major ordered that our trumpets be played, and we in our boats danced, and the Captain-Major too, along with us.'[2] But maybe the music was misunderstood, or it sounded too

The inhabitants of this country are tawny-coloured. …They are dressed in skins, and wear sheaths over their virile members. They are armed with poles of olive wood to which a horn, browned in the fire, is attached. Their numerous dogs resemble those of Portugal, and bark like them.

The South African coast, described by Alvaro Velho, *Journal of Vasco da Gama's First Voyage in Calicut*, 1498[3]

aggressive, and there was an armed stand-off, the Africans disappearing in a state of panic. There were to be many similar moments when the new arrivals copied the music that was demonstrated for them in this way. Both Columbus and Magellan did it, and it often led to the same stand-off as it did now.

DOM VASCO DA GAMA CONDE ALMIRANE QVE FOI O PRIMEIRO Q DO REINO VE IO COTI TOLO DE VIZOREI O:6:G DA ÌMDIA

Vasco da Gama took on the leadership of the expedition to India at the age of just twenty-six, after the unexpected death of his father.

The Hindus posed a serious categorization problem for Europeans used to designating people as either Christian or Muslim, which is how Vasco da Gama could end up worshipping by mistake at a Hindu temple. There were practical reasons why it made sense to be close to the Hindus. The Portuguese needed good relations with someone, to help those guarding the forts alone in the long winter months. It was with Hindu support that nobleman and naval officer Alfonso de Albuquerque took the city of Goa, only to lose it again in the truce between Hindus and Muslims. One complication was that the Muslims were often better merchants. 'They can do better calculations by memory than we can do with the pen,' said one Florentine merchant in 1510. 'And they mock us, and it seems to me that they are superior to us in countless things, save with sword in hand, which they cannot resist.'[4]

An Indian mosque and a Hindu temple in a 16th-century engraving: the European arrivals in India found the Hindu religion hard to categorize.

In southern Africa, all they could do was communicate in sign language, and that was always uncertain. But as Vasco da Gama's fleet proceeded up the eastern coast of Africa, there were at last some familiar means of orientating themselves. The first Arabic speakers emerged, which meant they could ask for local pilots (one of whom was whipped for his mistakes), though they kept their origins as Christian explorers secret.

In Malindi, on the Kenyan coast, they were sent what they believed was a Christian pilot, Ibn Majid. Historians have speculated that this may actually have been a very famous navigator indeed, the Arab geographer Shihab al-Din Ahmad ibn Majid al-Najdi, generously sharing his knowledge despite his premonition that it would mean the destruction of his world. In this way, Vasco da Gama finally crossed the Indian Ocean, to find a very busy trading environment, dominated mainly by Gujarati, Tamil, Persian and Arab merchants, and by a cacophony of different races, languages and shades of religion. When Vasco's small fleet anchored outside Calicut on the southwest coast of India on 20 May 1498, on the outskirts of the Mughal empire, there were as many as 700 other ships from all over the East as far as China. It was a defining moment in business and maritime history.

The Portuguese were sailing the first European ships in the Indian Ocean. They had discovered a laborious sea route to this huge market, and everything was difficult to judge. Even so, some aspects were very familiar. Obsessively careful, Vasco sent one of his convicts ashore, expecting extreme difficulties in translation. He brought back with him a Moor, speaking in Castilian and Genoese. 'Good fortune, good fortune,' he said. 'Many rubies, many emeralds! You should give many thanks to God for having brought you to a land where there are such riches!'[5]

The problem both for the pioneers and the locals was as usual: how to categorize the strangers. When Vasco finally went ashore a week later, with crowds of people watching him, he was taken to a Hindu pagoda that he was told was a church. Inside he saw what he believed was an image of the Virgin Mary and he fell on his knees. The Indians who flocked to see him were just as confused. These must be Near Eastern Muslims, surely. But why could they not speak Arabic and why were they wearing such peculiar clothes? In fact, it

FOLLOWING PAGES

A sumptuous depiction of Vasco da Gama's arrival in India, woven in silk and wool in the Tournai workshops in Belgium in the early 16th century.

was the attire that Calicut recalled for generations. They remembered their weapons and their armour, and the men who 'wore their hair long and had no beards except around their mouths'.[6]

Negotiations with the rulers of Calicut were difficult from the start. Local officials were afraid Vasco would sail away without paying port duties; other merchants were suspicious. Vasco was dismayed at the endless demands for more gifts and that he should hand over his rudders for security. He managed to extract something that looked like an agreement for trading rights but had to sail away under cover of darkness when he was told to leave his cargoes as collateral.

Here Vasco made a fatal and familiar mistake. When he set sail for home on 29 August, he ignored local knowledge about the winds, and found himself battling across the Indian Ocean against the monsoon. The journey took 132 days and half his men died, with many of the rest left weak with scurvy. The news of his achievement only reached Portugal a year later.

Vasco da Gama was overlooked for the critical return trip to the Indies. Instead, his place was taken by Pedro Alvares Cabral, who was given secret orders to take his fleet far out into the Atlantic, where – as

ABOVE A statue, kept by Vasco da Gama, was all that remained of the *São Rafael*, burned on the return voyage from India.

Part of Vasco da Gama's second fleet, which took him back to India in 1502.

expected – he encountered the South American continent, in what is now Brazil. When Cabral arrived in India it was clear that the representatives left behind by Vasco da Gama had been murdered. Cabral eventually bombarded Calicut and sailed south and, in accordance with another theme in the story of these encounters, found himself welcomed by Calicut's rivals in the small kingdom of Cochin, and was able to take holds full of gold and silk back to Europe.

Vasco da Gama made a second voyage to India soon after, sailing with twenty warships in February 1502. He seized a ship coming back

OPPOSITE Pedro Alvares Cabral landing at Port Seguro in Brazil, an event that marked the beginning of Portugal's empire in Latin America.

The Spice Islands (also known as the Moluccas) in the Queen Mary Atlas, commissioned by Queen Mary I of England as a gift for her husband, King Philip II of Spain, but published in 1558, after her death. It was presented to her successor, Elizabeth I.

from a pilgrimage to Mecca, stole the cargo and locked the passengers in the hold, before ordering it to be set on fire. A series of similar actions followed until he finally fought a full-scale battle in Calicut harbour, destroying the Calicut fleet of twenty-nine ships and finally getting the concessions he wanted. It was a policy known to historians as 'forced trade'.

Vasco da Gama's last journey to India was two decades later; he caught malaria and died in Cochin on Christmas Eve in 1524. By then, an inexorable logic was driving Portuguese expansion. They needed the east African coast, around what is now Mozambique, to support their voyages to India, which is how a Portuguese presence there began. Their policy of 'forced trade' implied pressing on aggressively eastwards, and they seized the Malacca Straits which led to the Spice Islands in 1511.

King Manuel was soon presiding over an expanding trading empire of the most enormous ambition and energy, and styling

Part of a Portuguese map of the coast of Brazil, dating to c. 1519, showing indigenous people harvesting brazilwood, used to make a simple red dye.

himself 'Lord of the Conquest, Navigation and Commerce of Ethiopia, Arabia, Persia and India'. It was a complicated business: Portuguese goods were bartered for pepper from Gujarati merchants, and this was used in the East Indies to get silver and cotton, which was used to buy Chinese goods. These were then used to procure Japanese goods. 'One thing leads to another,' said a Dutch governor in the Indies.[7]

The difficulty was that Portugal was too small a country to staff an empire in Brazil as well as the East, and to provide the leaders they needed when only one in ten of those who went to administer and trade in the empire ever returned home. Within half a century, the empire was already in decline, as the Dutch and then the English were struggling for their own toeholds in the East.

Chapter 2

Discovering America: Christopher Columbus

Four hours before Rodrigo de Triana first sighted the Americas, from the forecastle of the *Pinta* on 12 October 1492, the adventurer Christopher Columbus had seen something himself from the deck of the *Santa Maria*. It was just on the horizon, 'like a little wax candle rising and falling', he said, and then he saw no more.[1] At dawn that morning, as Columbus's ships edged into the bay of what is now thought to be Watling Island in the Bahamas, the first meeting with the naked Taínos who were on the beach at the time carried with it an almost supernatural sense of mystery. It was a flickering glimpse of another world.

We know so little about what they felt, those people who would be described for centuries as having been 'discovered', but we know from other encounters what it probably was: a sense of fear, awe and excitement, with an ambiguity about whether this was some kind of magical encounter. They must have watched as a man in coloured leather was rowed ashore with a huge flag, fell on his knees and, with these other demi-gods, conducted some strange ritual of possession. The newcomers called the island 'San Salvador'. It was only then that these men, if that is what they were, turned their attention to the astonished islanders and gave them red caps and glass beads 'and many things of slight value, in which they took much pleasure'.[2]

Like so many of the pioneers in this book, Columbus knew about being an outsider. His roots were unclear, though we know now that he came from Genoa and that his later voyages were financed by Genoese traders. But he remains a mysterious figure, both brilliant and incompetent, a religious maniac and an incomparable navigator,

Naked women found by Columbus, here shown in an edition of his 1493 letter describing his voyage, were a major source of fascination.

OPPOSITE Columbus's small fleet leaves for America in August, 1492.

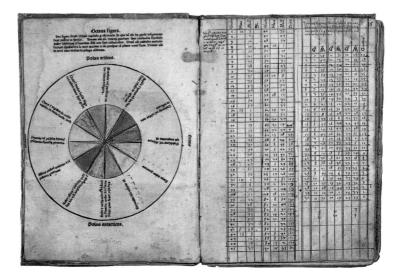

A compass alongside a table showing winds and light at different latitudes, on the pages of Columbus's own copy of *Imago Mundi*, which he may well have carried on his first voyage across the Atlantic.

a cruel persecutor and a humanitarian who was immediately inspired by the simplicity of the people he encountered.

We know Columbus had visited England at the end of a career as a corsair or mercenary, probably via Southampton and thence to Bristol. It was at this point that he must have made the trip to Iceland that he was to boast about later, sailing tantalizingly close to Greenland and the edge of the known European world. In Bristol, he witnessed the fifty-foot tides, a clue to the size of the Atlantic before him. In

Between the edge of Spain and the beginning of India, the sea is short and can be crossed in a matter of a few days. Christopher Columbus, marginal note in his own copy of *Imago Mundi*[3]

Iceland, he may well have heard stories about the old Norse settlements beyond in Helluland, Markland and Vinland. And in Galway on the way home, something happened which may have given him an idea. A small boat was towed in carrying a man and a woman, still alive after drifting for some time, both of them of 'most unusual appearance'. Columbus believed they were Chinese. Whether this provided the kernel of what became his obsession – sailing west to get to the East – or whether that was something else, we will never know.

By the time Columbus had persuaded the Castilian court to back him, he was alone in the enterprise – even his brother Bartholomew was at the French court at the time. The contract was signed, the ships procured and, on 1 August 1492, the *Niña*, the *Pinta* and the *Santa Maria* were ready. It happened to be the same day as the deadline for the Jews of Castile and Aragon to leave the country – a brutal side effect of the capture of Granada from the Muslims earlier in the year – and the roads were packed with refugees as Columbus made the final preparations. The ships carried provisions for a year, an Arabic translator and diplomatic letters addressed to Magnus Canus, the Great Khan, with some duplicates where the names had been left blank.

Columbus faced a revolt by his terrified crews just a few days before the great encounter between East and West on 12 October. They were afraid that, with such favourable winds, they would never be able to get back. But there was some unmistakable evidence of land close by: plants and sticks floating in the water. Then there was the mysterious light, and then the island, and the Taínos staring back. These weren't quite the Eastern potentates Columbus had been expecting.

Columbus's initial feeling was definitely a kind of love. 'No one would have believed it, who has not seen it,' he wrote. 'Of anything that they possess, if it be asked of them, they never say no; on the contrary, they invite you to share it and show as much love as if their hearts went with it, and they are content with whatever trifle be given them.'⁴ He believed he had encountered people in an innocent state. The tragedy of his achievement, and of his settlements in the Caribbean, was that the charm soon turned into a desperate frustration at the lack of gold, then brutal suppression and finally genocide.

It was to become the pattern of the relationship between the Old World and the New, in this case largely because Columbus's expedition was not so much exploration as investment. It had to make a profit. It eventually did so, but the basic problem was that Columbus was wrong about the sea route to China. His calculations were mistaken. He had underestimated the circumference of the earth by a quarter but still refused to believe it, even when it was clear to everyone in Europe that a vast new continent stood in the way.

Columbus was always close to the Franciscans, who were particularly concerned with the innocence of the natural world, and when Columbus saw that the Taínos were all but naked, innocence was what he believed it implied. But he also saw people who could be exploited. Columbus was a complex man, and these two sides pulled

No existing portraits of Columbus were painted in his lifetime, but this one – from Genoa – is said to have been a good likeness.

Columbus and Cabot

To what extent was what Columbus called his 'enterprise of the Indies' planned together with the Venetian and former Genoese merchant, John Cabot? That was what the historian of exploration David Quinn suggested, but it is impossible to prove.[5] Even so, their collaboration now seems by far the most likely interpretation. Both were originally Genoese, probably with connections to the pro-French Fregoso party and to the coastal port of Savona. They were almost exactly the same age. Their 'enterprises' were virtually identical, and so were their contracts, though Columbus in the end demanded more in return. Both were involved around the fringes of the wool and silk trade from southern Europe to Bristol and London. Both frequented the same ports, Lisbon and Huelva, also used by sailors from Bristol with the stories of exploration that must have filtered out of there. What is more, as it turns out, both ended up so heavily in debt in the mid-1480s that they had to leave their homes with their families and find somewhere else to live.

Cristoforo Grassi's view of the bustling port of Genoa half a century after Columbus and Cabot were born there.

The horror of cannibalism, as reported by Columbus and his successors, added spice to the published reports of explorations around the world. This French engraving dates from 1558.

him in almost opposite directions. For the Taínos, this magnificent new arrival and the small gifts he had brought seemed uncomplicated. They played in the sea and in canoes around the ships for the rest of the day. The first transatlantic encounter was a social success.

But for Columbus, this was also the high point. The rest of his life was a series of disappointments, many of which he simply refused to accept, beginning almost as soon as he reached the mainland of the large island he named Hispaniola (the inhabitants called it Haiti). There were no lions, elephants or camels, and it was clear that the Arabic translator he had brought with him was of no use at all.

Columbus took on board a number of Taínos, communicating with them in sign language and beginning to teach them Castilian. They could soon converse well enough to say why they were frightened as the voyage progressed. They explained that they were sailing into the territory of the Caribs – fierce people they described as having one eye and the faces of dogs – who were known to capture and eat them. On shore, Columbus's men were horrified to go into a hut and find a man's head in a basket.

This is another recurring theme: over and over again, the explorers came to believe the people they had encountered were cannibals (the word derives from 'carib'). When the Chinese and Portuguese encountered each other in the Far East, both sides believed the other ate human beings. What Columbus's men actually

FOLLOWING PAGES
German-American artist Albert Bierstadt's 1893 painting of Columbus landing on Watling Island, and the first known transatlantic encounter.

La Navidad, the tiny colony that Columbus established on his first voyage, from an edition of his 1493 letter to the king and queen of Spain.

saw is still controversial – and the reality of cannibalism remains disputed – but we know what they believed they saw, and there is evidence that some of the peoples of what is now Latin America occasionally ate their enemies. It was precisely the opposite of the idea of the indigenous people being innocent.

Columbus and the rest of the crew of the *Santa Maria* were exhausted as Christmas came near. There had been little moon and the curious Taínos had been climbing all over the ship for the previous two nights. In the early hours of Christmas morning, when the sea was dead calm, the *Santa Maria*'s captain Juan de la Cosa went to bed, leaving the ship's boy at the tiller. The ship slipped so gently onto a coral reef that at first nobody noticed. When it did become clear, part of the crew panicked and set off in a boat for the *Niña*. By the time they had been sent back, the coral had plunged holes into the hull and water was pouring in.

This must have been a moment of confusion for the Taínos as well. Suddenly, the strangers who had descended like gods were in need of assistance. In the early hours of the morning, the local chief Guacanagarí was woken with an urgent request for help. Through the following day, Guacanagarí and his people helped the crews rescue the stores and as much from the ship as they could before it broke up. They also helped to use the wood from the ship to build a fort. It was the first European settlement in the Americas since the time of the Vikings, and they named it after Christmas Day: La Navidad. Guacanagarí watched as the tower rose up, together with the first of the thatched huts that would form the basis of a new town. The *Santa Maria*'s crew were to be his neighbours.

'All the islands are so utterly at your highnesses' command that it only remains to establish a Spanish presence and order for them to perform your will,' Columbus wrote to Queen Isabella and King Ferdinand. 'They are yours to command and make them work, sow seed and do whatever else is necessary and build a town and teach them to wear clothes and adopt our customs.'[6]

For the Taínos, the mystery surrounding these new arrivals seems to have disappeared, perhaps with the loss of the *Santa Maria*. The newcomers' obsession with gold was just one of their peculiarities. They also had strange dietary habits, not valuing the small edible dogs that the Taínos consumed. They seemed ignorant of the business of producing manioc and cassava, and they ate prodigious amounts. The Taínos complained that the Castilians ate in a day what most of them ate in a month. The cruelty of the Europeans was almost as staggering, but that was to be an unpleasant discovery later on. The Taínos had begun by doubting the humanity of the new arrivals because they seemed supernatural; we know they were to come to doubt it again because of their sheer heartlessness. Columbus set off home with the *Niña* and the *Pinta*, his relations with the two captains strained to breaking point, and taking with him ten of the Taínos for another encounter in another world.

The admiral, for that was what Columbus had become, did not return to his islands until November 1493. He arrived with what seemed to be half the world offshore, with seventeen ships, 1,300 men, including colonists, cavaliers and friars, and instructions from Isabella to convert the natives and to treat them kindly.

But La Navidad was gone, its wooden walls blackened with fire and its inhabitants dead. A small faction among *Santa Maria*'s crew had roamed about the island stealing gold and women, and the

Three Taíno amulets, known as zemis, in the shape of gods. The Taíno had a complex religious system based on a hierarchy of gods of both sexes and in human and animal form, and believed that amulets provided protection.

islanders had exacted a terrible revenge. Guacanagarí was confronted and discovered to be lying about a wound to his leg (supposedly suffered while defending the people of La Navidad). He was forgiven, but the supposed culprits were soon hunted down, and relationships between the two sides were never innocent again. A more independent-minded chief called Caonabo was tricked into wearing handcuffs and sent back to Castile in chains.

Many others would follow him. In the absence of gold, Columbus decided to send the Taínos home as slaves. He sent out his men with their horses and dogs – which were known to terrify the locals – and rounded up 1,660 Taínos from all over the island. Of those, 550 of the healthiest men and women were loaded aboard ships. Of the rest, he told his men they could choose any that were left for themselves. Some 400 who remained even after that division were told to go. By the final leg of the voyage, half of the slaves had died, their bodies thrown overboard.

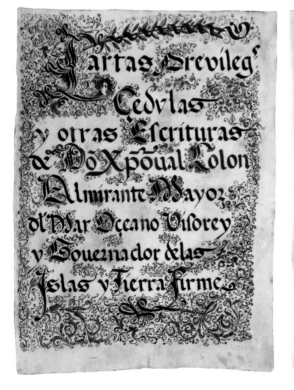

These events roused the Taínos across Hispaniola into action. The chief of all the chiefs, Guaniguana, united as many of the tribes on the island as he could in the early months of 1495 and advanced on Columbus's new city of Isabella to drive the Europeans into the sea. Columbus, along with his brother Bartholomew who had by this time arrived from Spain, led 200 soldiers out to meet them, and a combined charge of lancers with dogs terrified the Taínos and put them to flight.

But the slaves were never sold. Queen Isabella ruled that their enslavement was not legal, and they must be sent home. Few survived. This and the cruelty of the Columbus brothers to their own recalcitrant colonists led to a growing political clamour for his removal. In 1500 he was sent home from his third voyage in chains. Despite his fall from grace, Columbus was allowed one last expedition. He called

Columbus is clapped in irons for his cruel behaviour in Hispaniola.

Navigation

Mariners in the 15th century could judge latitude by the height of the Pole Star in the sky, but otherwise they largely relied on what is known as 'dead reckoning'. Columbus had his own version of this, based on his feel for the speed of the vessel and his sense of the wind and current. This also required a compass to judge direction, and was usually supplemented with a knotted rope, which was piled on the deck, attached to a float behind the ship, and allowed to pay out into the sea. Every change in direction and speed had to be marked in the 'log'. Columbus was one of the most effective navigators of any age, but was often swayed by extreme optimism and wishful thinking. On his 1492 voyage, he kept parallel charts – one to mark the ship's position and one to reassure the crew. The fake, conservative chart was actually much more accurate.

A navigator measures the height of the Pole Star in the sky: the angle between the Pole Star and the horizon equates to latitude.

---

it the 'High Voyage' and it was intended finally to break through to the Indies and to bring back enough gold to restore his lost titles. He ended up marooned on the beach in St Ann's Bay, Jamaica, in armed conflict with half his companions and awaiting rescue by his enemies in Hispaniola.

I...began to ponder this matter of the shape of the world. And I concluded that it was not round in the way that they say, but is of the same shape as a pear.

Columbus's thoughts on his third voyage about the shape of the planet, 1498[7]

Columbus's final years were spent in increasing ill-health, complaining bitterly about his poverty and his treatment by the sovereigns. He was not actually poor – the ship carrying his own gold had been the only one to escape a disastrous hurricane (a Taíno word) that had destroyed the returning fleet of his nemesis, Francisco de Bobadilla – but he felt poor. He died in Valladolid in northern Spain on 20 May 1506 aged only fifty-four, in a small house, looked

Insula Iamaica.

Franciscus Poraz.

Christophorus Columbus.

T4

A letter from Columbus to his son Diego, written in Seville in February 1505, mentioning the promise by explorer Amerigo Vespucci to intervene on his behalf.

after by the Franciscans, whom he had long admired. There was hardly any contemporary mention of his death.

By that time, it was already clear to everyone except Columbus that he had not actually found the Indies, but a 'New World' – the breadth of which was still unknown – which seemed to block the way. Vasco da Gama's successor, Pedro Alvares Cabral, had stumbled, not entirely accidentally, on the coast of Brazil. Columbus's friend Amerigo Vespucci, after whom the new continent was named, had sailed with a Portuguese expedition that reached as far south as Rio. The hunt was on for a way through to the Indies, via a northwest or southwest passage. This hunt was to dominate the next few centuries of exploration, and lead to more encounters between people, and the same misunderstandings and bloodshed that Columbus's confusion had led to, all over again.

OPPOSITE The battle between Columbus and his rebel captain Francisco Porras in St Ann's Bay, Jamaica, depicted by the 16th-century engraver Theodor de Bry.

Chapter 3

The Northwest Passage: John Cabot

Columbus's ambiguous relationship with the Taíno people was to lead to another extraordinary and historic encounter. The ten captives who had been taken back across the Atlantic in 1493 by Columbus found themselves, after a glimpse of the harbours in the Azores and Lisbon, walking down a narrow plank of wood in the small port of Palos de la Frontera, from where Columbus had set out seven months before. From the plank they were immersed straight into medieval Europe, with its smells, its horses, its tall houses and churches, its colour and excitement. There were also unexpected dangers, including the fearsome prospect of the unseen: germs were even then devastating the Taínos on both sides of the Atlantic.

After two weeks of rest, Columbus set out with his ten captives for Seville, arriving on Palm Sunday. He wanted to see the sovereigns of the newly united nation, Ferdinand and Isabella, to show off the wonders of what he insisted were the Indies. John Cabot, the Italian navigator and explorer who may well have been Columbus's frustrated former partner, was in Valencia at the time and must have seen him, standing like a Roman senator, proud and unsmiling, with six of his captives around him. The prisoners were almost naked, wearing as much gold and finery as Columbus could find, each of them carrying a brightly coloured parrot in a cage. Everything brought back in triumph from the expedition was on show: hammocks, pineapples, iguana skins and gold masks.

Historians have imagined that this encounter must have been the moment Cabot decided to press on with his own voyages to the

The departure of John Cabot from Bristol in 1497, painted in the Bristol City Museum.

OPPOSITE Columbus in Barcelona before Ferdinand and Isabella in 1493: Cabot may well have seen him in Valencia, on his way north.

Indies. He had been to Mecca; he knew these men with parrots were not from the East. Did he conclude correctly that Columbus had not, in fact, made it to Asia? Did he realize there was still an opportunity to sail across the western ocean and reach the East along shorter northern latitudes? Or did the doubts gnaw away more slowly. Either way, little more than three years later, Cabot had letters patent from King Henry VII of England giving him and his sons rights over any lands he discovered that were 'unknown to all Christians' – the formula the English used to defend against accusations from Castile that they were trespassing.

We know Cabot was born in Genoa and that he moved to Venice at the age of eleven. There is a tradition that he was actually born in the mountain village of Castiglione Chiavarese, about 30 miles (50 km) down the coast towards La Spezia. Here, near the castle and Benedictine abbey – deep in wine and olive country – a ruined house is still known as the birthplace of 'Giovanni Caboto'.

If the 'enterprise of the Indies' had originally been a joint venture with Columbus, it would imply that Cabot's mysterious journey to Mecca in the mid-1480s was undertaken to discover more about the sources of Eastern goods. As it was, this or some other venture left Cabot heavily in debt. He tried to dig his way out by

The 1496 letters patent to John Cabot and his sons, authorizing voyages in search of unknown lands.

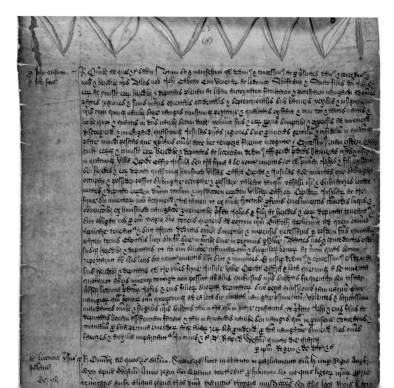

The Northwest Passage

When the navigators in the 1490s had established that a huge land mass blocked the direct crossing from Europe westwards across the Atlantic to China, there was speculation about what routes – if any – might allow a passage all the way through. This was especially important for traders in northern Europe, because the Pope had assigned the western Atlantic to Spanish navigators and the east to Portuguese. The Northwest Passage was the dream which drove the English, in particular, to seek out the way through the Arctic and into the Bering Strait. For five centuries they pushed further in, often with great loss of life. This included the ill-fated expedition led by Sir John Franklin in 1845, which led to the disappearance of himself and his crews. Only in 1906 did Roald Amundsen make the voyage successfully between Greenland and Alaska, and it has been repeated many times since. In 1997, it was reported for the first time that global warming had opened the way through the Northwest Passage without an icebreaker.

Franklin's ill-fated expedition presses on through the ice in search of the Northwest Passage through the Arctic.

The full-size replica of the *Matthew* built in Bristol in the 1990s for the 500th anniversary of Cabot's voyage.

permanently disposing of some of his wife's dowry, and in return agreed with her family to sign over the rights to all his property in Venice – the results of his years in the property business. It was clearly not enough.

For more than a decade, Cabot and his family wandered around the courts of Europe, on trading voyages to Bristol or in Milan, Savoy or eventually Valencia, always one step ahead of the creditors. He chose Valencia because it was the centre of the cloth and skin trade in the Mediterranean, which was his primary expertise, but also because there were possibilities for other kinds of development. There are still records in existence of Cabot's negotiations over a major harbour-building programme there. It was also a potential base from which he could plan and equip an 'enterprise of the Indies' all of his own.

It is significant that Cabot had spent time in Bristol. There is evidence that there had already been a series of secret expeditions from there, seeking out the mythical island of hy-Brasil on the other side of the Atlantic at the same latitude. There may also have been sightings by Bristol fishermen, operating illegally off the Newfoundland coast (by agreement with Denmark, they were not supposed to be there). When Cabot set sail on 2 May 1497 on board the tiny *Matthew*, on what was his second attempt to cross the ocean, his backers or his crew may have had some knowledge of what was out there.

On 23 June, the crew sighted some birds, a sign that they were near land. They were also astonished at the plentiful cod, thick in the sea wherever they looked. That night, there was the unmistakable odour of fir trees. At 5 a.m. the next morning, St John the Baptist's day, they saw an island ahead. Cabot named it St John and moved on. Just a few hours later, more land was visible on the horizon, and this time it looked like the mainland, with enormous forests and a beach where a landing could be made.

Rival historians have battled for centuries about where the land that Cabot named 'Prima Terra Vista' or 'Land First Seen' was, whether it was Cape Bonavista or Cape Breton – whether in Newfoundland, elsewhere in modern Canada or in Maine, or even further south. The Canadian consensus is that he landed somewhere in what is now Newfoundland, though that name, 'New Founde Land', was previously applied to almost anywhere along that coast. Wherever it

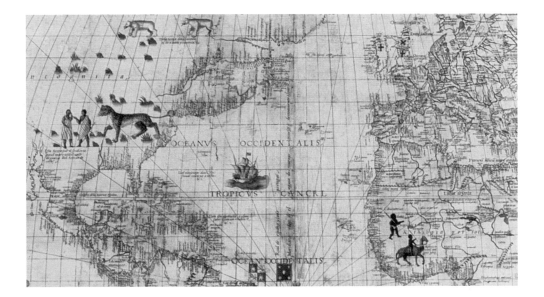

was, Cabot launched a small landing boat carrying three banners representing England, his native Venice and the Pope.

    There was a path from the beach and a track which had clearly been made by humans. They quickly found a snare and an old camp fire, and what looked very much like an arrow and a needle. They looked up at the enormous trees, tall enough for the masts of ships, and peered into the dense undergrowth. But this time, there was no encounter. Perhaps because of the risk of being surprised on the beach, Cabot decided to leave and press on with the business of exploring the coast, after which he headed home.

John Cabot's son Sebastian's 1544 map of the world, showing the western coast of North America.

That Venetian of ours who went with a small ship from Bristol to find new islands has come back and says he has discovered mainland 700 leagues away, which is the country of the Grand Khan, and that he coasted it for 300 leagues and landed and did not see any person.

Lorenzo Pasqualigo, Venetian merchant writing home about Cabot's 1497 voyage[1]

    Back in London, he was granted a pension and bought himself a silk outfit. But what Columbus had achieved, and Cabot had patently not, was a title. Perhaps this is why he allowed himself to become known in London society as the 'admiral' – an Arabic word without a formal use in English at the time. Having constructed a map and globe to demonstrate where the New Founde Land was, and how he thought it connected to the Indies, Cabot put them on display and gave a series of public lectures. Both the map and the lectures were also ammunition in the war of words with Castile. It demonstrated where he had gone and set out the official English view: that Cabot had not been, and was going nowhere near, Columbus's discoveries.

A year later, Cabot made a return trip to North America with five ships, one of which turned back after damage in a storm. He then disappears from formal history, and most historians have believed until recently that he disappeared at sea. But there is peculiar evidence to the contrary.

Browsing through a junk shop by the Seine in Paris in 1832, the Dutch ambassador Baron Charles Walckenaer came across an ancient map. It was damaged and crumbling, and in an irregular shape since it was painted on oxhide. When unrolled, it was 1.8 m (6 ft) long. There was an inscription on the bottom which said it had been made in 1500 by Juan de la Cosa, the former captain of the *Santa Maria.*

Juan de la Cosa's world map, made in the New World before news of Vasco da Gama's voyage had arrived, but which includes information that may have come from Cabot himself.

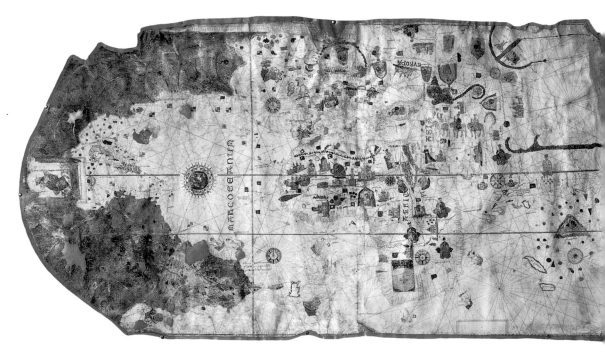

It transpired that the map had been in the Vatican archives when they were raided by Napoleon in 1810 for a new library in Paris. Most of the booty was returned to Rome later, but this map was mislaid. Walckenaer took it home, and it was bought by the Spanish government when he died in 1853. It is now in the Maritime Museum in Madrid. The reason the map is usually accepted as genuine is because, although it is the first of its kind to show the entire American coastline, it does not yet incorporate information brought back from Vasco da Gama's voyage to India. But it is the details that are interesting.

Some way up the North American coast – it is hard to work out quite how far, because there is no Florida – there are two sets of English flags with the legend *mar descubierto por inglese* ('sea discovered by the English'). The places marked along the North American coast also include names like Cape de Inynglaterra and St Nicholas – also the patron saint of Bristol's mariner's church. These features all imply some connection with Cabot, though they are hard to decipher. By itself the map is no proof, but there are other signs that de la Cosa seems at some point to have exchanged information with Cabot or one of his companions. This confirms rumours and snippets of evidence that Cabot and some of his 1498 fleet made contact with the Castilians in the Caribbean. This would have been a threat to the interests of Castile and a bitter disappointment for Cabot. They were still nowhere near China.

It then emerged that the historian of exploration Alwyn Ruddock, who died in 2005, had found evidence that Cabot did indeed encounter the Castilians and that he came back to Bristol alive. In the early 1990s, Ruddock had been commissioned to write a book to celebrate the five-hundredth anniversary of Cabot's landing, and rumours had been filtering through the exclusive world of Cabot research that she had made staggering discoveries in some newly uncovered archives. But she was dissatisfied with the book, tore it up, started again and never finished it; she stipulated in her will that all her notes and research should be destroyed after her death.

After Ruddock's death, the historian Evan Jones published an article based on her original book proposal, which set out some of what she had found.[2] The real bombshell was that Ruddock believed she had evidence that Cabot had reached Newfoundland in 1498,

Juan de la Cosa, pioneer map-maker and the master of the *Santa Maria*.

Manuel I, the Portuguese king who licensed rival expeditions to the Arctic.

European iron artifacts were used and often modified by Beothuk Indians. These items were excavated from a Beothuk living site in central Newfoundland.

leaving a party of friars there. They established a church and religious colony while Cabot and the fleet sailed south along the coast towards the Caribbean and the encounter with the Castilians. The friars organized their own expedition to Labrador, perhaps with help from a new 1499 expedition licensed by Henry VII, and Cabot himself struggled back north again in the autumn of 1499, reaching England early in 1500.

The tragedy for Cabot was that the climate at Henry VII's court was very different in 1500 compared to eighteen months before when he had set sail. Negotiations for the marriage between Henry's son, Arthur, Prince of Wales, and Isabella and Ferdinand's youngest daughter Catherine of Aragon were in full swing. Nothing would be allowed to upset the delicate new relationship between England and Spain. A few months later, Cabot was dead.

The Portuguese had been disturbed by news of Cabot's 1497 expedition, convinced that his 'New Founde Land' was probably Portuguese under the Treaty of Tordesillas (1494), which drew a line down the middle of the Atlantic dividing the world between Castile and Portugal. The solution was to journey there themselves and stake a claim. The Portuguese King Manuel's main thrust was still to India, but in 1500 he licensed two rival expeditions, both setting out from the Azores and heading northwest.

The first was led by John Fernandes, from the Azores, the so-called labrador or 'yeoman farmer', who came across an icy coast later that year which was probably Greenland. The second was led by a nobleman, Gaspar Corte Real, also from the Azores. Gaspar's father John Vaz Corte Real had made a famous voyage westwards in 1472 and may even have sighted Newfoundland. He was also well connected to other explorers: he was a cousin of Columbus's wife Filipa and was related by marriage to an old rival of Columbus, the German explorer Martin Behaim.

Some time in the summer of 1500, Corte Real's expedition to the northwest encountered a mountainous cape, which he described as a 'point of Asia', but was actually Cape Farewell, the southern tip of Greenland. The aristocratic Corte Real had been given better terms than Fernandes and his partners, who therefore shifted their allegiance to Bristol. In 1501, Fernandes was given letters patent by Henry VII, which reveals something about the attitudes towards indigenous peoples at the time. There is a passage in it that appears in no similar document, charging them to punish those 'who rape or violate against their will or otherwise any women of the islands or countries aforesaid'. The only parallel was Isabella of Castile's injunction to treat the Taínos kindly. Both Fernandes and Gaspar Corte Real seem to have died early in their exploring careers, but their rival consortiums carried on the struggle.

To Portungales that brought popyngais & cats of the mountayne with other stuff to the King's grace. Entry in an account book recording payment by Henry VII of 100 shillings for animals from the 'Newfound Island'[3]

Also interested in the far north was Cabot's son Sebastian, who seems to have believed he had glimpsed the opening of the hoped-for Northwest Passage through the Hudson Strait in 1508, a secret which became deeply uncomfortable for him when he was working for the Spanish. Henry VIII's expedition to find it, led by William Hore in

Sebastian Cabot as an old man. This image has often been wrongly identified as a portrayal of Sebastian's father John.

1536, ended in disaster. There was an encounter with the Inuit, who fled, and Hore's failure to learn about Arctic survival from them led to terrible hunger. Some of his men resorted to cannibalism, which was ironic given that evidence of cannibalism among the Native Americans further south was used as the justification for any number of atrocities.

When the English began the search in earnest, under Martin Frobisher, the Portuguese policy of seizing locals was practised increasingly, and it proved a huge attraction back home. Crowds came out to see the captive Frobisher brought back from Baffin Island in 1576, who survived for a week. Some of the horror of this from the point of view of the Inuit is revealed by a story from Frobisher's later trip, when he lured a man on board with a bell and grabbed him. Frobisher hoped, as one might expect, that the man could learn to interpret for them, but 'for very choler & disdain he bit his tongue in twayne within his mouth'.[4]

Frobisher took a man, woman and child back with him to England in 1577, after an encounter at what became known as Bloody Point. The couple actually turned out to be unrelated, though they were still accommodated in Bristol as if they were married.

Arnaq, the Inuit woman taken to England by Frobisher in 1577.

Dutch fishmonger and artist Adrian Coenen was inspired by depictions of Frobisher's 1576 Inuit captive in a pamphlet, and in the late 1570s included this drawing in his extraordinary *Fishbook*.

OPPOSITE John White's painting of Frobisher's revenge on the Inuit at Bloody Point after the disappearance of some of his men.

Verrazzano and Cartier

Giovanni da Verrazzano, sailing for the French, is credited with exploring the coast of what is now the United States in the 1520s, while his former crewman Jacques Cartier explored the coast of Canada in the 1530s and 1540s, and began the historic link between North America and French culture. It was Cartier who borrowed a Huron-Iroquois word to coin the name 'Canada'. Cartier's encounters with the Iroquois followed the usual pattern, from astonishment and trade and then – despite his determination to avoid violence – outright kidnap. Yet in Cartier's career we can find one of those few moments of learning and co-operation. During the winter of his second voyage, his crew was desperately ill with scurvy. It was the arrival of one of his former captives, Domagaya, who explained to him a medicine made from a local tree that could cure scurvy. So few expeditions before or since learned anything from the people they encountered, but Cartier did and the medicine saved his expedition.

Cartier visiting the Iroquois village of Hochelaga on 3 October 1535, depicted in a book by his contemporary Giovanni Battista Ramusio.

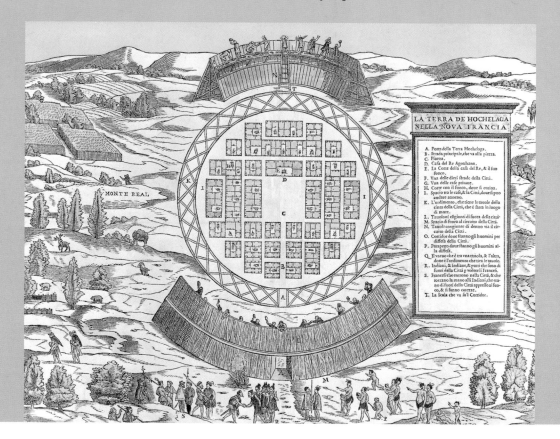

A 1710 engraving showing how the fishing industry was being established in Newfoundland.

Kalicho, the man, demonstrated Inuit hunting on the Avon to a huge crowd, but later died from complications relating to a broken rib. Before he passed away he sang the same death song he had sung as he left his homeland. The woman, Arnaq, showed no emotion at his graveside, but died four days later. Nutaaq, the child, died of measles shortly afterwards.

Christopher Hall, chief pilot on all the Frobisher expeditions, described the Inuit as being like Tartars, 'with long black hair, broad faces and flat noses, and tawny in colour, wearing sealskins; and so do the women; not differing in fashion; but the women are marked in the face with blue streaks down the cheeks, and round about the eyes.'[5] The evidence, handed down through the generations, is that the main reaction of the Inuit was astonishment about what the new-comers were wearing: how could they possibly keep warm?

The future of these icy northern shores lay, in the end, not with the dreams of eastern gold that had motivated Columbus and Cabot, but with the teeming seas. The cod and later whales that frequented these seas would eventually earn the gold and silver that the Spanish were bringing back from the New World, and would form the basis of the British empire in America.

Chapter 4

Circumnavigation: Ferdinand Magellan

Cabot and Columbus may have failed dismally to find China by sailing west, but by the time they died – Cabot in 1500 and Columbus in 1506 – they had posed a geographical puzzle that the next generation of explorers risked their lives, time and time again, to unlock. Its solution was a critical element in European high politics at the beginning of the 16th century, just as it was a problem involving the best geographers, map-makers, diplomats and spies. It was also a problem in two parts: what was on the other side of this land mass that seemed to block the way to China from the Arctic to the Antarctic, and was there a way around it?

It was a stowaway fleeing from creditors who finally solved the first part of the conundrum. Vasco Núñez de Balboa, the leader of an attempt to settle in the region of Darién in what is now the border area between Panama and Colombia, sent an enthusiastic letter home to Isabella of Castile's husband Ferdinand in 1513, accompanied by a consignment of gold. In the letter, he even used the overblown phrase 'rivers of gold'. Faced with this temptation, the royal court agreed to finance their first expedition since 1493, under a seventy-year-old soldier called Pedro Arias de Ávila, known as Pedrarias. As soon as Balboa heard the news that Pedrarias was on the way, he realized he would have to find these 'rivers of gold' himself.

He marched inland in September 1513, through an exhausting succession of swamps and jungles, attempting to build alliances with those he encountered. This was the policy the Portuguese were beginning to adopt in the East, using the divisions they discovered

Vasco Núñez de Balboa takes possession of the Pacific Ocean.

OPPOSITE Magellan was the first European to encounter the natives of the Mariana Islands in the Philippines, shown here in the Boxer Codex, *c.* 1595.

there to provide themselves with support, safe passage and eventually local forces at their disposal. It was also the policy of Columbus's rebellious colonists, who made common cause against him with factions of the local Taínos. Balboa enforced these alliances by brutal retaliation against representatives of tribes he encountered who would not help, having them torn apart by dogs.

Heading up the first mountain peak, he reached the summit on 25 September 1513, and saw finally the sight which had eluded Columbus. Stretching into the far distance was another blue ocean to parallel the Atlantic. Balboa raised his hands and saluted the sea, then he marched down to the edge of the ocean, waded into the water wearing his armour until he was breast deep and raised his sword, taking possession of it in the names of King Ferdinand of Aragon and his daughter Joanna of Castile.

The second half of the puzzle was how to sail to this new ocean. It was increasingly clear that there was no passage through Central America, but there was huge speculation among the Portuguese, English and French about a Northwest Passage through one of the many river mouths that had been discovered in the north. There was similar speculation among the Spanish about the gigantic rivers that might perhaps lead to a Southwest Passage. The Spanish watched with horrified fascination as the Portuguese advanced, island by island, on the pivotal Spice Islands in what is now Indonesia, so this question became increasingly important. The quest to find a Southwest Passage was the project that would eventually give Ferdinand Magellan a place in the history books.

Magellan was actually Portuguese, born to impoverished aristocratic parents in 1480. He was one of those wounded in 1506 in a battle between Portuguese nobleman Francisco de Almeida and a huge fleet of 200 ships from Calicut. He sailed home with Ludovico di Varthema, the extraordinary Italian traveller who had originally swum out to Almeida's flagship to warn him of the attack. Varthema had been to the Spice Islands, and by the time they were back in Lisbon, he was dreaming of the riches of the East, and had developed a plan to buy pepper direct from the Spice Islands rather than from middlemen who could control the price.

By 1509, Magellan was in the Spice Islands himself, building his reputation as a courageous soldier but a difficult subordinate.

Ferdinand Magellan, a bolder adventurer than this 17th-century engraving of him suggests.

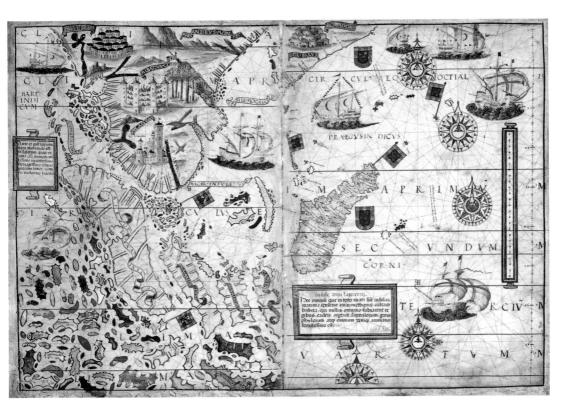

A page from a c. 1519 Portuguese world map, charting the early discoveries of the Portuguese in the East Indies, where Magellan made his name. This world map, part of which is also shown on p.35, represents the entire known world just prior to Magellan's circumnavigation.

King Manuel disliked him and when the two men met in 1515, and Magellan demanded another commission from him, it led to a peculiar and historic stand off. If he no longer wanted his service, Magellan asked, would the king allow him to serve another country? Manuel said he hardly cared. A year later, Magellan offered his services to the Spanish, explaining that he knew the whereabouts of a Southwest Passage.

It has never been quite clear where Magellan got this idea from. The Spanish expeditions to the south had been closely guarded secrets. Amerigo Vespucci may have gone as far as the River Plate, the huge estuary of which separates modern-day Uruguay and Argentina, and which had seemed a likely prospect for a route through to the Pacific. German maps at the time, probably drawing their information from the unreliable Martin Behaim, did mark a Southwest Passage. But whatever Magellan thought he knew, he

Spices

Spices, including pepper, cinnamon, nutmeg, cumin and ginger, were the great luxuries of the medieval period. They were used as food preservers and medicines and for a range of other vital purposes, and they contributed enormously to the rise in power and wealth of Venice. The fall of Constantinople to the Turks in 1454 changed all that, by cutting off Venice and Genoa from the main trade routes from the East. When Vasco da Gama sailed to India, around the Cape of Good Hope, he opened up a new route by which these spices might make the journey to Europe, and Portugal then set about securing the sea routes to and from India. Once the Portuguese had control of Goa in 1510 and Malacca in 1511, they could trade directly with China. But Columbus and the other pioneers in the New World also discovered a series of new spices, including chilli, chocolate and vanilla, which launched a new spice trade with the Americas.

A 1542 representation of a red chilli pepper; by this time chilli pepper cultivation had spread from Mexico to the Philippines and India.

SILIQVASTRVM
TERTIVM.

Langer Indianischer Pfeffer.

convinced the young emperor, Charles V – who had inherited the thrones of Ferdinand and Isabella – to invest in his voyage. He was given five unseaworthy ships and a crew of criminals. It took him a year to repair them and make the expedition ready.

Magellan set sail from Seville on 10 August 1519 with supplies for two years. There were immediately disputes with his crews, one of the perennial problems for these pioneers. At the height of a storm off the coast of what is now Uruguay, he shouted at his crew: 'We cannot go back here, because this is as far as Vespucci arrived. We have to go beyond.'[1] His relationships with his captains were even

ABOVE The young Holy Roman Emperor and Spanish king, Charles V, a few years before he agreed to back Ferdinand Magellan's voyage.

One of the *c.* 1522 'Brixen Globes', this one terrestrial and the other celestial. Along with some other globes and maps which pre-date the end of Magellan's voyage, it suggests that passage might have been possible around the southern tip of South America.

A fantastical portrait of Magellan on his voyage of discovery, as imagined by Theodor de Bry a century afterwards.

more difficult. They were Spanish and resented being under the command of a foreigner. Magellan dealt with the situation by putting the captain of the *San Antonio* in chains. The fleet reached the River Plate on 10 January 1520.

As the weeks went by, it was increasingly clear that the search was hopeless. Magellan continued the voyage southwards and braved it out with the captains, realizing that any alternative strategy would probably lead to his own arrest. At the end of March, he announced that they would spend the winter in the Bay of St Julien in southern Argentina and that the rations would have to be halved. Two days later, he faced a determined mutiny involving three of his five ships. From the *Trinidad*, he managed to trick his way onto the *Victoria*, stabbed the captain and used the ship to block the harbour. When the *San Antonio* dragged its anchor, and drifted against him, Magellan and his men stormed aboard and took control. One captain and his chaplain were marooned and left to their fate. Another was beheaded, and his servant and foster brother pardoned on condition that he dealt the blow.

Up until this point, Magellan had had few encounters with indigenous peoples. He had reached the conclusion that the region where he planned to spend the winter was actually uninhabited. Then, a few months after the abortive mutiny, a gigantic warrior with a red-painted face and bow and arrows appeared on the cliff and began a strange dance aimed in their direction. Magellan told one of

Immediately the sailor led this giant to a little island where the captain was waiting for him; and when he was before us he began to be astonished, and to be afraid, and he raised one finger on high, thinking that we came from heaven. Antonio Pigafetta describes meeting John the Giant in Patagonia, 1519[2]

the former mutineers to make their way over to him and to copy his movements. This time, it was the right decision. He came aboard and asked, using sign language, whether the ship had come from the sky. He also commented on how small Magellan's crewmen were compared to the size of the ship. The word Patagonia – 'land of the clumsy feet' – stems from a comment by Magellan at this encounter recorded by his private secretary and diarist for the expedition, Antonio Pigafetta.

A 1606 map of southern South America, marking Patagonia and including a Patagonian 'giant' holding a bow and standing next to a European for scale.

The crew christened the warrior 'John the Giant', and discovered that he was terrified of mirrors and fascinated, as Columbus's Taínos had been, by the little hawk's bells they carried with them. He entertained them by putting a sharp arrow down his throat and pulling it out again without injuring himself. Here was one more successful encounter that did not quite last. Magellan and his men were fascinated by the giant's colleagues, and followed John into the forest to his village. They found nothing of value there, but the temptation to take some of these people back with them became overwhelming.

Two young warriors were lured onto the ships, given leg irons to play with, and were told they were decorative. When they were riveted to the deck, they roared in rage, and John the Giant gathered a raiding party, which failed to secure their release, but did some damage with their poisonous arrows. Once the prisoners had calmed down, they turned out to have huge appetites, drinking water by the bucketful and even eating some of the ship's rats. One died shortly after the fleet set sail.

On 21 October, Magellan's fleet finally reached what turned out to be the narrow, rocky passage that still bears his name. The fleet

A 17th-century map of the Strait of Magellan showing Dutch explorer Joris van Spilbergen's journey through the strait in 1614. He went on to circumnavigate the globe. Even though almost a hundred years had passed since Magellan's death, only a handful of other round-the-world voyages had been completed by this time.

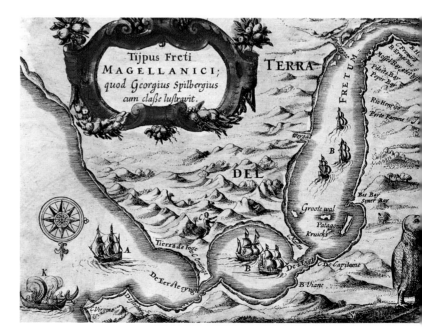

avoided destruction in a hurricane and then edged their way carefully through 375 miles (600 km) of misty and dangerous crags, constantly battered by the weather. Food was also getting dangerously low when the crew of the biggest ship, the *San Antonio*, finally overpowered their captain and headed for home, taking the one surviving Patagonian with them. A month later, the others emerged from the storms of the Cape and headed west into a blue expanse they called the Pacific, and with it a whole new challenge. The sun was blinding. The water ration was down to a sip a day. Every rat was hunted down to eat. The crews even ate the leather covers off the yards. Finally, on 6 March 1521, after ninety-nine days at sea, there were clouds on the horizon, which meant that land could not be far away.

The island turned out to be Guam. Here and on nearby Rota, Magellan came to the conclusion that he had missed the Spice Islands of the Portuguese and was heading towards China. He also ran into difficulties with the locals. They stole everything they could, even the ship's skiff on his flagship, the *Victoria*. In response, Magellan took forty armed men ashore and burned some of the houses, killing seven, but rescuing the boat.

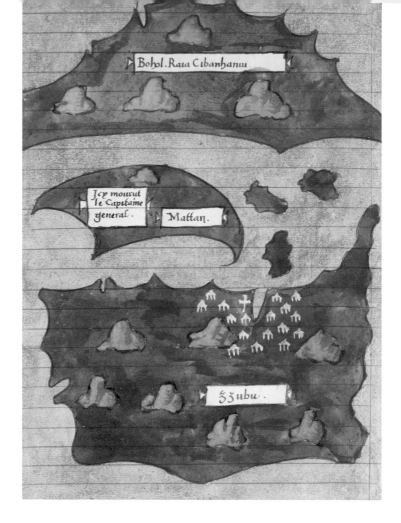

The islands of Bohol, Cebu and Mactan, where Magellan met his own fate, from the French edition of Antonio Pigafetta's record of the journey.

The next set of islands, where Magellan and his crew were able to recover from their Pacific ordeal, he dubbed the Lazarus Islands – the place where, like Lazarus, they came alive again. Later in the century they were renamed after the Spanish crown prince, who would one day be crowned Philip II, so they have been known since then as the Philippines. On 28 March 1521, on the small island of Lima Sawa, he had his breakthrough moment. Magellan had been sailing with a slave from the Spice Islands, called Enrique, who spoke Malay. At all their stopping places, he had tried to converse with the inhabitants, without effect. Here, finally, he was understood. The local people watched expectantly, and Magellan floated presents to them on a plank. In return, the chief sent him a bar of gold. Magellan tactfully refused it, but the next day – Good Friday –

After we sailed from that island, following our course, and those people seeing that we were going away followed us for a league, with a hundred small boats, or more, and they approached our ships, showing to us fish, and feigning to give it to us. Antonio Pigafetta in the Pacific, 1521[3]

he and the chief went through a ceremony of blood brotherhood. It was one of those rare moments of equality and hope in the story of European exploration, but it wasn't to last.

On the nearby island of Cebu, he organized a mass baptism of 800 locals, promising not to use any kind of force to persuade them to take part. But the chief of the neighbouring island of Mactan was hostile and refused to recognize Magellan or his claims. Magellan was taken aback and did not want to let this challenge to the power of Spain go unanswered. He organized a punitive expedition there, and was offered men by the local chiefs who urged him not to lead the expedition himself. He rejected their advice. On 26 April he took fifty men onto Mactan and immediately found himself surrounded by 1,500. When he was hit by a poisoned arrow, he managed to order a retreat but he was not able to save himself. The retreat quickly turned into a headlong flight, and his body was left behind. 'They had killed our mirror, our light, our succour and faithful guide,' said Pigafetta. 'Even when they had wounded him, he kept turning to the shore to see whether we had reached the boats safely.'[4]

The usual pattern whereby the European newcomers allied themselves with the disaffected neighbours had reversed itself. Magellan had fallen victim to the latter this time, and the discovery that the Europeans were mere mortal men led to further trouble for the remaining fleet. Magellan's slave Enrique refused to work for anyone else. When he was threatened, he went on shore and warned the people of Cebu that the Spaniards were planning an attack, urging them to strike the first blow. As a result, twenty-five of Magellan's men were killed at a banquet on the island. The fleet now only had 114 men left, which was not enough to man all three ships. They decided to set the *Concepcion* on fire and abandon it.

Cebuano islanders in the Boxer Codex, c. 1595; they killed twenty-five of Magellan's men at a banquet.

An encounter in the Mariana Islands, from the Boxer Codex, c. 1595.

The surviving members of Magellan's crews were now desperately hungry and terrified of further bloody encounters. The rest of the journey was a nervous affair, the men firing indiscriminately on any ships that came near, leaving anchorages behind by cutting through their ropes, and usually too frightened to land. Finally, they reached the Spice Islands on 6 November 1521. It was the edge of the world known to Europe, but also a kind of treasure trove. 'Cloves, sago, ginger, coconuts, rice, almonds, bananas, sweet and sour pomegranates, sugar cane, nut and sesame oil, cucumbers, pumpkins and pineapples – an extraordinarily refreshing fruit

about the size of our water melons – could be found here,' wrote Pigafetta, 'as well as a peach-like fruit called guava and many other edible plants.'

They bought as many spices as they could, and sold clothes to buy more. The leaky *Trinidad* then headed home via the Strait of Magellan, but was captured by the Portuguese and interned, and only a handful of the crew ever made it home. The remaining ship, the *Victoria*, was now under the command of the Basque, Juan Sebastián Elcano, who had been one of the mutineers. He set sail in the other direction. Three months later, he refused the entreaties of the crew

The *Victoria*, from Flemish cartographer Abraham Ortelius's 1589 map *Descriptio Maris Pacifici* ('Description of the Pacific Sea').

Prima ego velivolis ambivi cursibus Orbem,
Magellane novo te duce ducta freto.
Ambivi, meritoq̃ vocor VICTORIA: sunt mî
Vela, alæ; precium, gloria; pugna, mare.

BELOW Juan Sebastián Elcano, who captained the *Victoria* and her remaining crew on their exhausting final leg around the world.

to leave them at the Cape of Good Hope, on the grounds that it was Portuguese. When he finally struggled into Sanlúcar de Barrameda near Cadíz in southern Spain, on 6 September 1522, only eighteen men remained alive to tell their extraordinary tale.

The spices left in the *Victoria*'s leaky hold were valuable enough to pay for the whole voyage. But the crew was disconcerted to find that they had apparently lost a day during their circumnavigation. We now have an International Date Line which makes these things explicit, but their main concern was that they must have inadvertently celebrated the Christian holy days on the wrong dates.

Elcano died three years later trying to repeat the voyage along the same route, but the real problem was that Magellan – like Columbus before him – had been mistaken. The Southwest Passage that he identified was too far south to be of any practical use, and the Pacific was just too gigantic. The Spanish could not use it to compete with the Portuguese for access to the Spice Islands of the Far East.

There followed a series of attempts to sail west from the emerging Spanish empire in Latin America. The famous conquistador Hernán Cortés sent ships west from Mexico in 1527, but they were never seen again. More mutinies, wrecks and disappearances followed over the next decade. It was not until 1565, nearly half a century after Magellan, that Miguel López de Legazpi made it back to the Philippines, via the Marshall Islands, and founded a European colony there. His pilot, Friar Andrés de Urdaneta, solved another part of the puzzle by finding a route back to Mexico in a wide northward sweep, where he encountered prevailing westerly winds that could take him home.

While this was going on, there was a parallel vision being hammered out back in Spain among the geographers. The consensus was that the Pacific was not quite as empty as it might have seemed to Magellan, and that lurking somewhere in the south was another vast

This *c.* 1542 map by Battista Agnese, prepared for Charles V as a gift for his son, traces Magellan's voyage in black.

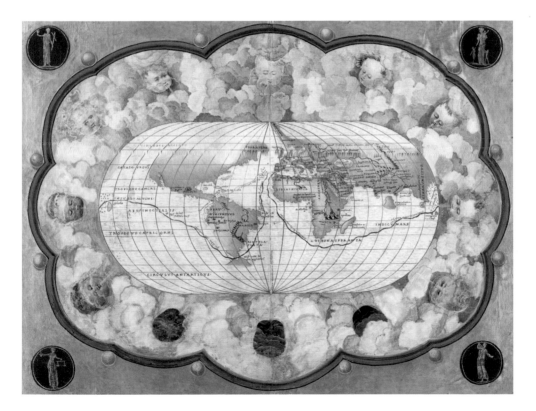

Mendaña

Álvaro de Mendaña de Neira's encounters with Pacific islanders in the 1560s took a familiar and depressing course. On island after island, starting in the Solomons, they began with the usual astonishment and desperate search for categories by which each side could understand each other. There were often good relations to start with, until the need for fresh water and food began to overwhelm the resources of whichever community they had arrived in. There were then the familiar stories of cannibalism. In the Solomons, where the islanders' pigs became the object of great competition, the locals are supposed to have offered Mendaña instead 'a quarter of a boy with the arm and hand' which he was urged to eat.[5] Then there were the usual misunderstandings, thefts and retaliations. It was all very predictable. Mendaña was back in 1595, sailing a small fleet from Peru together with his wife and most of her closest family, with the objective of founding a colony in the Solomons. Precisely the same patterns of encounters followed in the Marquesas Islands. Once more, the initial admiration of these graceful people turned to frustration and then violence. After two weeks, about 200 locals had been killed. Mendaña died that same year and handed over command to his wife.

A putona or shell trumpet from the Marquesas Islands.

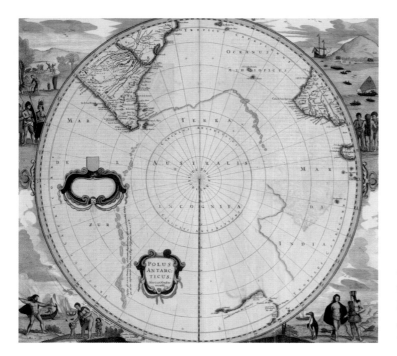

A 1642 Dutch map of the South Pole by Hendrik Hondius, showing 'Terra Australis Incognita' or 'Unknown Southern Land'.

continent. It was a dream that would last for two centuries, until the voyages of James Cook. So when a Spanish soldier called Pedro Sarmiento de Gamboa arrived in Peru in 1557, and began hearing the local Inca stories about lands of gold which lay further to the west, there was an academic audience prepared to listen to him. Sarmiento himself was furious not to be able to command the resulting expedition, but that role went instead to the governor's nephew, Álvaro de Mendaña de Neira, one of the most important Pacific explorers.

The pattern set by Spanish explorers was mirrored in the pattern set by the Portuguese. The two pioneering European nations had been kept apart by a line drawn down the Atlantic in 1494. Within a generation, the two sides had encountered each other around the other side of the world, and the islands and territories in between were beginning to be divided up amongst them – together with the people who lived there. It was to be centuries before this process was complete and, by then, the Dutch and then the English had intervened in the Far East. The next phase of exploration was to be one of colonization.

Xaltelolco.

Chapter 5

Exploiting the New World: The Conquistadors

Magellan was inching his way through the strait that now bears his name when the encounter of all encounters took place, between the Spanish adventurer and conquistador Hernán Cortés and Moctezuma, the emperor he was to overthrow to take control of large parts of Central America. It was an encounter not so much between supposedly learned and advanced Europeans and prehistoric culture, but between two kinds of sophistication, and it began with the edgy and nervous arrival of Cortés and his tiny band of followers in Tenochtitlan – on the site of what is now Mexico City – at the heart of the powerful Aztec empire.

There was Cortés, the supreme opportunist. There was Moctezuma, a hereditary semi-divinity surrounded by crowds and canoes on the huge lake that linked the different parts of the great Aztec city. The two men had been playing a game of cat and mouse with each other, Cortés slowly advancing via Moctezuma's small vassal kingdoms, Moctezuma discouraging the advance without taking action to prevent it, unsure – as so often in this story – whether the new arrivals were men or gods. When they finally met, Moctezuma descended from his litter under a canopy of feathers and walked towards Cortés supported by two lords.

'As we approached each other, I dismounted and was about to embrace him,' Cortés wrote later. 'But the two lords in attendance prevented me with their hands, so that I might not touch him.'[1] Cortés had been in Mexico for ten months and had gathered some translators along the way, not least of whom were Gerónimo de

Quetzalcoatl, the white serpent god. Moctezuma believed Cortés was Quetzalcoatl himself.

OPPOSITE Cortés with his Indian interpreter, La Malinche, from the 1585 *History of Tlaxcala*.

Aguilar, a shipwrecked Spanish priest who had learned Mayan, and the captive Doña Marina or La Malinche, who would eventually bear Cortés a son. So when Moctezuma spoke, Cortés could understand what he said.

'O lord, our lord, with what trouble, what fatigue, have you journeyed to reach us, have arrived in this land, your land, your own city of Mexico, to sit on your mat, your stool, which I have been guarding for you this while,' said Moctezuma. He still believed, as did most of those watching, that this was an encounter with the gods. To be specific, he believed Cortés was Quetzalcoatl, the white serpent god who had been predicted to arrive that very day and year. 'Your vassals, the old kings, my ancestors, are gone, after they too had kept ready your mat,' Moctezuma went on. 'Would that one of them could rise from the dead and astonished, see what my eyes truly see, for in no dream do I see your face.'[2] He promised to escort Cortés and his companions to his father's old palace, and led the way. The crowd watched silently.

It is easy to dismiss this encounter as wholly dishonest on the Spanish side. But in fact the Spanish came to admire Moctezuma,

An Aztec picture of their ritual of human sacrifice, from the mid-16th-century Codex Magliabechiano.

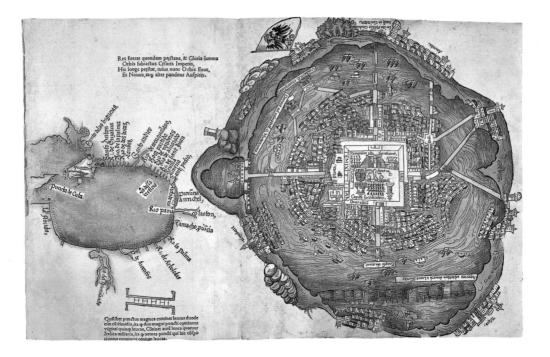

Res fuerat quondam prystans, & Gloria summa
Orbis subiectus Cæsaris Imperio,
Hic longe præstat, cuius nunc Orbis Eous,
Et Nouus, atq; alter panditur Auspicijs.

Quilibet punctus magnus continet leucas duode
cim est dimidia, ita q̃ duo magni puncti continent
viginti quinq; leucas, Cõtinet autẽ leuca quatuor
Italica milliaria, ita q̃ omnes puncti qui hic cõspi
ciuntur continent centum leucas.

and Cortés explained that he did indeed come from the sunrise, but that he was the subject of a great emperor. He and his colleagues were stunned by the size of the city before them, but the true immensity of it would have to wait for four days, as they were left alone in the old palace, wondering what to do next. Finally, Cortés was asked to go to the round earthwork at the north of the city. Moctezuma was waiting for him with his closest advisors at the top, next to sacrificial stones which were still drenched with the blood of two young men who had been killed that morning. Cortés and his men were horrified. They were soon to discover that the dead bodies from the sacrifices had had their hearts cut out, and then been rolled down the pyramid, where the limbs were given to the priests and then cooked. Supposed evidence of cannibalism had a habit of appearing at this point in the encounters.

Moctezuma took Cortés's hand and showed him the huge market below, the hubbub from which was already reaching them, and the huge cities along the edge of the lake. He pointed out the public toilets – no such thing existed in Spain – and the whole of

Tenochtitlan, one of the largest cities in the world at the time. Its sheer size and complexity staggered Cortés and his men.

The banner with the image of the Virgin Mary carried by Cortés and his men during their march to Tenochtitlan.

Tenochtitlan, four square miles with perhaps 300,000 inhabitants. There were huge palaces, fountains and zoos, causeways, grid patterns of canals and gardens. Its four sectors were each dominated by a temple, and a huge cement aqueduct delivered drinking water across the city. It was bigger than anything in Europe, and one of the largest cities in the world at the time.

The Aztecs were at the height of their powers. They had never seen a horse or discovered the wheel, except to drive children's toys, but this was civilization of a kind that most of those in Cortés's party had never dreamed of: terrifying, bloody, but hugely impressive. This was the land they had been sent, all 600 of them, to conquer.

The truth was that Cortés needed to make something happen. He was a minor aristocrat from Medellín in western Spain and had become a magistrate and secretary to the governor of Cuba. In 1518 he was appointed Captain-General of a mission to secure territory in inland Mexico for colonization. But at the last minute he was recalled from this expedition by the governor and had ignored the message. He needed a huge success to avoid being punished as a mutineer.

It was a period of massive expansion for the empire. Jamaica had been invaded in 1509. Cuba had been conquered by an expedition that included Cortés two years later. Juan Ponce de León had scourged Puerto Rico with terrible bloodshed, nearly wiping out the indigenous population. Cortés initially had only a few hundred men with him. The first pitched battle with the locals resulted in a number of women prisoners, all of whom then converted to Christianity, and one of whom was to become famous as his mistress and advisor, La Malinche. She knew the weakness of the Aztec empire and advised Cortés just how hated and feared Moctezuma was by the outlying kingdoms and fiefdoms who paid him tribute. It was a recipe for the usual pattern, whereby the new arrivals would achieve the leverage they needed in alliance with one of the warring groups they found.

The Florentine Codex illustrates La Malinche's conversation with an Aztec with speech scrolls.

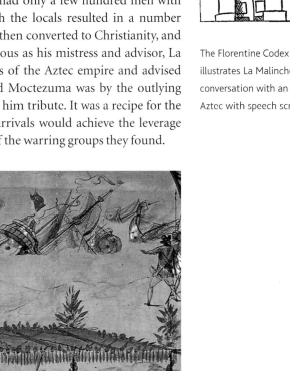

Cortés dining with two of Moctezuma's envoys, soon after landing at Veracruz.

The massacre of the Aztec nobles in Tenochtitlan's main temple complex by Pedro de Alvarado.

He met some of Moctezuma's emissaries in Veracruz, as the emperor played for time, unsure what kind of arrival this represented, and turning down Cortés's constant requests for a meeting. He sent lavish gifts as an ineffective method of holding the Spaniard at bay. Cortés and his men marched exhaustingly through the mountains and the terrible heat of the jungle to the city state of Tlaxcala, which immediately agreed to an alliance. By the time Cortés arrived in Tenochtitlan in November 1519 he was accompanied by a powerful army, with a few horsemen and cannons, but with many hundreds of allied troops collected along the way. Moctezuma had believed, mistakenly, that if he led Cortés to the heart of the empire, and he turned out to be dangerous, he could crush him. It was not to be. After the initial meetings, Cortés, with just thirty armed men, entered Moctezuma's palace and took him captive along with his family, and demanded that he swear allegiance to the Spanish emperor Charles V. Throughout the game of cat and mouse, Moctezuma had been paralysed with indecision, unable to read the portents and incapable of resistance.

So far, Cortés had managed his mission with huge nerve and inspiration, and some cruelty. When he heard that a large and hostile

Spanish force had arrived on the coast, he left 200 men behind and marched to confront this new threat. He daringly captured the leader of the Spanish troops (who then joined Cortés), only to find that the situation in Tenochtitlan had begun to unravel. His lieutenant, Pedro de Alvarado, had massacred some of the locals in the main temple

The Spanish attacked the musicians first, slashing at their hands and faces until they had killed all of them. The singers – and even the spectators – were also killed. This slaughter in the Sacred Patio went on for three hours. Aztec eyewitness account of the massacre which led to the uprising against Cortés[3]

complex, and there was an immediate rebellion. Cortés dashed back and there followed the events of what came to be known as the Noche Triste, which marked the end of the Aztec empire.

It was now 30 June 1520. As the fighting spread below them in the city, Cortés asked Moctezuma to use his influence to bring calm. Moctezuma told him he would not be able to, because the people below had chosen another emperor and had sworn not to let any of

In this contemporary portrait by German artist Christoph Weiditz, Cortés holds the coat of arms created for him as first Marquis of the Valley of Oaxaca.

the Spanish live. 'I believe you will die in this city,' he said. Then, protected by Cortés's men, he went out onto balcony, only to be hit by three stones and an arrow. He died in Cortés's arms. Cortés fought his way out of city and by dawn two thirds of his men and all their local allies had been killed, and they had lost all their artillery and their looted treasure. Moctezuma was succeeded by his nephew Cuitlahuac, who reigned for just eighty days before dying of smallpox (a disease imported by the Europeans).

Cortés laid siege to the city once reinforcements had arrived, subduing its allies and cutting off supplies, reducing the inhabitants to eating lizards and rats. By the following summer, he had built 1,600 boats for the final assault and the city fell on 13 August 1521, six months after Magellan's death in the Philippines. The last pretender to the throne, a young man called Cuauhtémoc, was caught by the Spanish and was eventually hanged for his involvement in a plot against them. A terrible thunderstorm accompanied the fall of the city. Tenochtitlan was renamed Mexico City and, for the next three years, Cortés was its governor.

Throughout his advance and his attack, Cortés had played on Aztec confusion about him, and their fears that his arrival represented some kind of supernatural event. Horses were unknown in America and now, as before in Hispaniola under Columbus, their presence compounded the mystery. Cortés led the Aztecs to believe that the horses went into battle of their own free will; those who

Cortés at Texcoco on the eastern shore of the lake of the same name, where he went to finish construction of the fleet that would enable him to attack Tenochtitlan from the water.

A horse being lowered into the waves from a Spanish ship moored off the coast of the Gulf of Mexico.

opposed them could not see whether the riders and the horses were separate beings. The result was not just the destruction of the Aztec civilization, but also of one of the world's most extraordinary cities. 'I knew not how to free ourselves without destroying their city – the most beautiful city in the world,' wrote Cortés.[4]

The annexation of Mexico was one of the great turning points of history. Up until then, the energetic excursions of the conquistadors had island hopped across the Caribbean and into Central America, with yet more encounters with indigenous peoples and increasingly brutal extraction programmes to find the wealth that Columbus had promised. Some gold had been forthcoming, but not quite on the scale envisaged. But Mexico was different. Its gold wealth was on a scale none of the conquistadors had seen before.

An Aztec gold bracelet, part of a treasure found by an octopus fisherman in 1976 near Veracruz in the Gulf of Mexico.

Along with silver from the mines of Potosí and Zacatecas, huge amounts of precious metal were soon pouring back to Spain.

Cortés was part of a new class of adventurer for whom there was the possibility of huge rewards for those with boldness and nerve, but also the probability of death from disease or from the predatory hustle for power among their contemporaries. Vasco Núñez de Balboa, who had first glimpsed the Pacific, was beheaded in 1519, a victim of his successor, Pedro Arias de Avila. The man who arrested him was an illegitimate adventurer called Francisco Pizarro who had been in the New World since the days of Columbus. He was rewarded by being appointed magistrate of the new Panama City, and began the first of a series of expeditions towards the south.

There then followed a series of rumours, and small discoveries of riches further to the south, all of which fed into the growing legend of El Dorado. A measure of Pizarro's determination to find the mythical city came at the point of failure of his second expedition. When the new governor of Panama ordered him home, and sent a ship to pick him up, he drew a line in the sand. 'There lies Peru with its riches; here, Panama and its poverty,' he told his men. 'Choose, each man, what best becomes a brave Castilian.' Only thirteen stayed with Pizarro.

It was not until April 1528 that Pizarro, reinforced by his allies, finally reached the Tumbes region of Peru. They had a warm welcome from the locals – who called them 'Children of the Sun' because of their fair skins and bright armour – and were the first Europeans to see llamas. They also saw the first evidence of gold and silver. When he reached the heart of empire on his third expedition,

For when, either in ancient or modem times, have such great exploits been achieved by so few against so many; over so many climes, across so many seas, over such distances by land, to subdue the unseen and unknown? Francisco Xeres, secretary to Pizarro, reports on the discovery of Peru[5]

Pizarro was refused an audience with the Inca emperor Atahualpa, whose army of 80,000 soldiers massively outnumbered the newcomers. But Pizarro tricked and overwhelmed Atahualpa and a smaller force at the battle of Cajamarca in November 1532. Atahualpa was taken captive and, although he filled a so-called 'ransom room' with gold and silver, he was executed the following

The Incas

The Inca empire began its expansion less than a century before Pizarro's arrival, and was already tearing itself apart when he arrived. But it was impressive. The last survivor of Pizarro's expedition, Don Mancio Serra de Leguisamo, described in his will how the Incas organized their society virtually without crime. The road system stretched for over 3,000 miles, and the Incas had also developed agricultural methods that suited what was a mountainous region, with well-irrigated terraces cut into the slopes. It was the first civilization to cultivate potatoes. They also used a system of freeze-drying for storing potato crops. They had no iron or steel, but had developed a sophisticated bronze which they used for armour.

The Inca fortress and terraced fields of Písac in Peru. The terraces are still in use today.

July on a charge of murdering his brother. Pizarro's foundation of Lima followed in 1535, but inevitable disputes with his colleagues eventually led to his assassination in 1541. Pizarro's last words were 'Come, my faithful sword, companion of all my deeds!'

Cortés, meanwhile, had been exploring the Pacific coast of Mexico, venturing as far north as California. His contemporaries, like Hernando de Soto (southern USA), Pedro de Alvarado (Guatemala) and Juan Ponce de León (Puerto Rico and Florida), were making names and fortunes in other parts of the continent. The precious metals were flooding into Spain, making it staggeringly wealthy, but – in the process – destroying its productive economy and paving the way for its competitors in a generation's time. In the century that followed, 90 per cent of the trade between America and Spain was in precious metals. In the decade from 1550, a staggering 60 tons of silver and 8.5 tons of gold was shipped across the Atlantic.

More disturbing was the increasingly brutal nature of the encounters between conquistadors and conquered. The *encomienda* system, where a Spanish settler was granted land and a specified number of native people from whom they could extract 'tribute' in various forms, began with Columbus, after the failure of his taxation system. Cortés introduced it to New Spain, as the Spanish territories in North America were known. He was also one of the first people to try growing sugar in the Americas, and to import African slaves to help him do it, which was to have a massive effect on the future world.

Cortés recognized how cruelty by his lieutenants was causing some of the uprisings and rebellions that had to be so brutally suppressed. Alvarado's march to Guatemala was characterized by plunder and torture, and by the smallpox that followed. But the *encomienda* system was, in its own way, almost as brutal. It meant that the land itself was parcelled out to new owners by grateful conquistadors, and that those who lived on the land were included in the deal. Like Russian serfs, they were 'owned' by the landowner. It allowed a systematic kind of exploitation.

Like Columbus and Magellan, Cortés and Pizarro were meeting people who had no previous conception of their existence. Like Vasco da Gama, they were encountering sophisticated cities and markets they never expected before. But for the conquistadors,

OPPOSITE Theodor de Bry's engraving of Pizarro's arrest of the Inca King Atahualpa in 1532.

This drawing from the Florentine Codex, c. 1540–85, shows people suffering from the smallpox epidemic that afflicted Tenochtitlan in the years following the conquest.

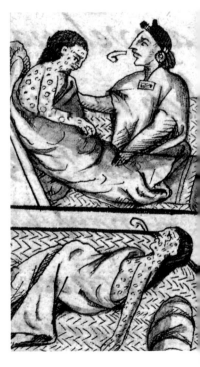

The Dominican Campaign

In 1511, the Dominican friar Antonio de Montesinos delivered his first sermon in Hispaniola, in a large thatched church at the centre of Santo Domingo that they were using as a temporary cathedral. 'This voice says that you are in mortal sin, that you are living and may die in it, because of the cruelty and tyranny which you use in dealing with these innocent people,' said Montesinos. He had watched the treatment of the Taínos with mounting horror for over twelve months. 'Are these not men? Have they not rational souls? Are you not bound to love them as you love yourselves?' At the end of sermon, he walked straight out of the church.

Montesinos was sent home and Ferdinand of Aragon, appalled by what he had heard, called together a group of theologians to meet in the Casa del Cordón in Burgos. One professor of law dismissed the Indians as 'animals who talk'.

Among those who heard Montesinos's first sermon was Bartolomé de las Casas, a future radical voice on behalf of the indigenous peoples.

A Dominican friar, Domingo de Santa Maria, with the Aztecs: the Dominicans were a powerful force for humanitarian reform.

each of these elements was pushed to an extreme. Cortés had seen and conquered a city that was bigger and wealthier than any in Europe. Pizarro had overwhelmed a culture so sophisticated that it had built a road stretching from Quito in Ecuador all the way to Santiago in Chile, with staging posts at regular intervals and suspension bridges across gorges. There was a growing campaign, led by the Dominicans, for kindness towards the indigenous peoples of the Americas, but it was bizarrely counter-productive, leading – among other things – to rules and conditions for conquest. This was the so-called *Requerimiento*, read to villagers usually in a language they could not understand. It was often used in a symbolic way, spoken to empty fields by the newly arrived conquerors. It was read to a deserted village in Darién by the conquistador Pedrarias in 1514, to the huge amusement of his colleagues. The great tragedy of the campaign to protect the 'Indians' was that, in relieving the demands upon them by their new rulers, it led to the beginning of the African slave trade to the Caribbean and Americas, which would come to dominate the political future of North America.

A drawing of two of the Aztec acrobats brought back by Cortés from the New World. The artist Christoph Weiditz saw them on a trip to Spain in 1528–29.

Chapter 6

The South Seas: James Cook

It was 23 April 1770, and James Cook was making what is the first recorded direct observation by Europeans of the indigenous people of Australia, walking along the beach near Bawley Point in New South Wales. 'They appear'd to be of a very dark or black Colour but whether this was the real colour of their skins or the C[l]othes they might have on I know not.'[1] Six days later, he and the crew from his ship, the *Endeavour*, landed on the continent in a place he called Botany Bay.

The locals were from a tribe known as the Gweagal, and the encounter continued along predictable lines. Most of them fled when the ship arrived, but a few stayed on the rocks threatening Cook's approaching boats with spears and pikes. There was a stand off, and then some gunfire. One of the warriors was injured and the party from the *Endeavour* landed on the beach where, just eighteen years later, the criminal flotsam and jetsam from the streets of London would be sent to found a new punitive colony. Joseph Banks, Cook's botanist, collected up forty or fifty abandoned spears on the beach. Four of these are still in existence, kept at Trinity College, Cambridge; their ownership is disputed.

So far, the encounters seem to have proceeded along a similar path to those between Magellan and the people of Tierra del Fuego or between Columbus and the Taínos. It is not clear what the locals thought of James Cook and his men, though their behaviour suggests they knew him to represent some kind of threat. There is a tradition that, like others before them, they believed the Europeans

A portrait of an aboriginal man decorated for a funeral ceremony. Cook's voyages included a number of artists.

OPPOSITE James Cook meets his fate on the beach in Hawaii, as portrayed by Johann Zoffany in c. 1795. The incident is still controversial more than two centuries later.

to be supernatural visitors representing dead ancestors. In fact, 'Captain Cook' has become a symbolic, slightly villainous figure in aboriginal mythology, whose gifts they fling into the sea.

But there was one difference with Columbus. Cook had on board a Pacific islander called Tupaia as navigator. The previous pioneers were in the habit of seizing locals to act as guides, interpreters and pilots. In this case, Tupaia not only begged to join the expedition, but he played a key role in it. Tupaia had met Samuel Wallis's English expedition in 1769, which arrived in Tahiti for the first time thinking it was part of the postulated southern continent, the existence of which Cook was about to disprove. They called him Jonathan, and he had been the lover of the woman Cook describes as the queen of Tahiti, Oborea. He was a wise man in his own culture, and was later welcomed by the Māori in New Zealand as a *tohunga*, a spiritual leader. Cook was initially sceptical about taking Tupaia, but he made him a map of all the Pacific islands he had visited, and some of his drawings remain in Banks's collection. Of all the intermediaries in the history of encounters, Tupaia was closest to an equal – though not among the *Endeavour*'s crew, who regarded him as a good deal too proud.

Tupaia's drawing of a longhouse and canoes in Tahiti, made when the *Endeavour* arrived there during Cook's first voyage.

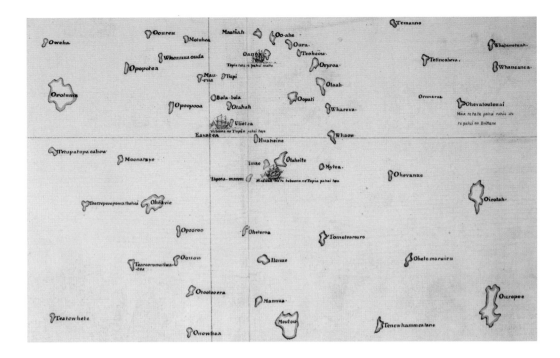

Tupaia's map of the Pacific islands: it was a map like this one that convinced Cook to take him further on the voyage.

So many of the great pioneers described in this book had been outsiders – Columbus, Cabot and Magellan were all sailing for nations other than their own, and were the object of suspicion among their crews and contemporaries. The conquistadors, almost by definition, were minor aristocracy or younger sons who wanted adventure, and needed it if they were to carve out any kind of role for themselves. James Cook, born in a small Yorkshire village in 1728, the son of a farm labourer, was no different. Fed up with his life as a shop boy, he had joined the merchant navy as a teenager, through connections with some ship owners in Whitby. He sailed with them on a series of coasters carrying coal out of the River Tyne.

It was at this point that Cook noted that his ambition was to go 'farther than any man has been before me, but as far as I think it is possible for a man to go.'[2] He joined the Royal Navy in 1755. But it was only when he mapped the entrance to the St Lawrence River, allowing General Wolfe to make his attack on Quebec in 1759, that the Admiralty took notice and commissioned him for the first of his Pacific voyages. He had been asked by the Royal Society to go to the Pacific to

James Cook, shown here in a miniature watercolour painted not long after his death, was a determined and straightforward man, but he became increasingly exhausted and irritable.

watch the transit of Venus across the sun; he was also given secret instructions by the Admiralty to see if he could find the missing southern continent. Alexander Dalrymple, the navy's chief hydrographer, was chief proponent of the idea of this huge landmass, and its existence or otherwise was the most debated topic in geography.

Terra Australis Incognita, the 'unknown southern land', had fascinated explorers back to Columbus and Vespucci. There was a sense that the balance and shape of the world somehow demanded one. It had become an article of faith over the centuries since then, though there was precious little evidence for it. The Dutch navigator Abel Tasman had made a similar journey to Cook's 120 years before, and no European had so much as laid eyes on New Zealand since then. Tasman had circumnavigated Australia in a wide sweep, pinpointing its vague position but little else. But this was not enough to stifle speculation about the continental land mass that Tasman must have missed.

Cook was aware of the fearsome reputation of the South Seas. Tasman had lost crewmen there. Cook's predecessor, Wallis, had been attacked in Tahiti and was forced to make an aggressive landing. When Cook arrived, in April 1769, he anchored cautiously in Matavai Bay, having crawled around Cape Horn. The *Endeavour* was a tough converted collier, but it was slow. To Cook's surprise, his arrival was actually welcomed by the locals and he began to set up an observatory on the shore to watch the transit of Venus, which ended up being the least successful aspect of his first Pacific voyage.

The South Sea islanders were enormously generous wherever they went, but there were two facets of the relationship with the locals that particularly concerned Cook. He turned a blind eye to the sexual encounters – which were such a central, but unremarked, feature of the business of exploration. But he knew that Wallis in the *Dolphin* had been worried about the number of nails being extracted from the ship's timbers to pay for sex, since iron nails were a valuable commodity on the islands. He was also worried about the pilfering;

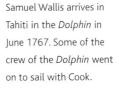

Samuel Wallis arrives in Tahiti in the *Dolphin* in June 1767. Some of the crew of the *Dolphin* went on to sail with Cook.

Matavai Bay in Tahiti, from where Cook watched the transit of Venus, the main purpose of his first voyage. This watercolour was painted shortly after Cook's return.

the islanders were extremely generous, but they expected the Europeans to be the same.

Cook was forced to act when a valuable quadrant went missing. His technique on these occasions, and it was the same when two of his crew went missing with their girlfriends, was to come ashore and seize the local chiefs, holding them hostage until the items or people had been returned. It was effective, but it would eventually lead to his death.

It was becoming clear that Cook was no ordinary navigator. He had packed the stores with fresh fruit, fresh meat, onions, wine and rum. He flogged two men for refusing to eat fresh meat and insisted that everyone ate sauerkraut. This policy was so successful

When we came into the Straits of Magellan we found it necessary to allow the ship's company a breakfast extraordinary when sellery could be got, as the Scurvy had just begun to appear; for, then, the stomach is in such a state it requires something of light and easy digestion.

James Cook, *Journal of the First Voyage*, 1769[3]

that not only was his voyage less affected by scurvy than any previous expedition, but also sauerkraut became so popular on board that it had to be rationed. By the time the masthead lookout sighted New Zealand in October 1769, it was clear that the voyage was going to be important.

Sex

Sex as an unspoken perk of the pioneering life is a neglected area of study. It was how Columbus's first expedition could bring virulent syphilis back to Europe. It was why a later charter for Cabot's successors by Henry VII of England carried a warning against forced sex. It was the nakedness of the indigenous people that first excited major interest among European audiences in Vespucci's writings, real or fake. And it was the real meaning of the description by Columbus's friend Michele de Cuneo of his encounter with a native woman. 'Having taken her into my cabin, she being naked according to their custom, I conceived a desire to take pleasure,' he said. 'I wanted to put my desire into execution but she did not want it and treated me with her finger nails in such a manner that I wished I had never begun.'[4] The Algonquin people who met Italian Giovanni da Verrazzano's expedition in 1524 made sure than no women went on board his ships. They knew the score by then.

Poedua, a local princess from Raiatea in the Society Islands, was taken hostage by Cook for the return of two deserters.

The Māoris who encountered Cook for the first time may have associated him with fairy folk who came from the sea. Like Moctezuma in Mexico, they were also influenced by a prophecy: a holy man called Titahi from a tribe living where Auckland is now predicted that huge changes were on their way, brought by new people bringing new kinds of control. The first encounters were therefore dangerous and violent. On the first attempt, ashore near what is now Gisborne, hostile Māoris on the other side of the river tried to cut off part of the landing party. One was shot. Tupaia's appeals that they came in peace were not effective. In Hawke's Bay, there was an attempt to kidnap Tupaia's servant. But Tupaia did manage to broker more peaceful meetings, aware that Polynesian navigators, known as the Te Rangi Hiroa, had been exploring the Pacific for some centuries before. The Māori chiefs who came aboard further north drew maps of the North Island in charcoal on the deck of the *Endeavour*, and Cook himself is remembered fondly in Māori oral tradition.

A dogskin cloak from New Zealand, brought back by Joseph Banks from Cook's first voyage and given to Christ Church college, Oxford.

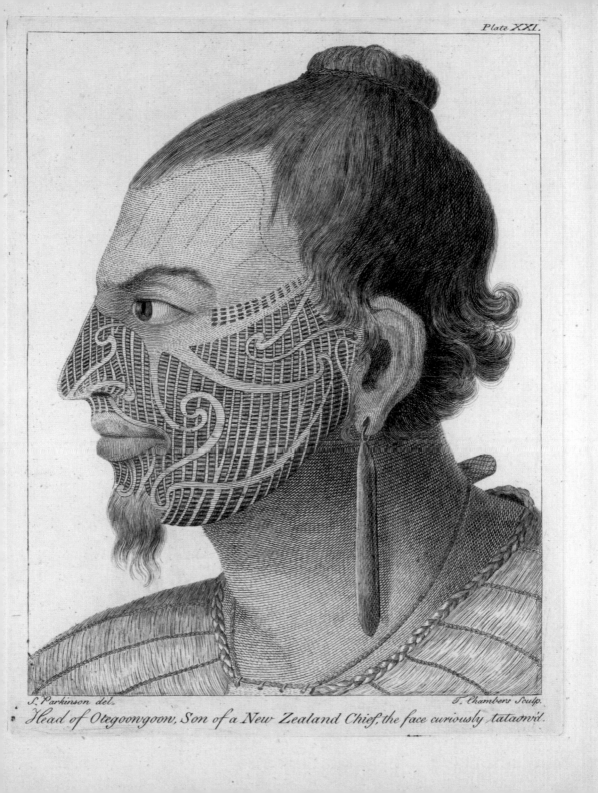

Plate XXI.

S. Parkinson del.

T. Chambers Sculp.

Head of Otegoongoon, Son of a New Zealand Chief, the face curiously tataow'd.

Tupaia's drawing of a Māori bartering a crayfish with an English officer.

But here we can know a little more, because one of those who was there for Cook's visit in 1769 was alive to have her impressions recorded seven decades later: 'We lived at Whitianga, and a vessel came there, and when our old men saw the ship, they said it was an atua, a god, and the people on board were tupua, strange beings or "goblins". The ship came to anchor, and the boats pulled on shore. As our old men looked at the manner in which they came on shore, the rowers pulling with their backs to the bows of the boat, the old people said, "Yes, it is so: these people are goblins; their eyes are at the back of their heads; they pull on shore with their backs to the land to which they are going"…These goblins began to gather oysters, and we gave some kumara, fish, and fernroot to them. These they accepted, and we began to roast cockles for them; and as we saw that these goblins were eating kumara, fish, and cockles, we were startled, and said "Perhaps they are not goblins like the Māori goblins".'[5]

The Europeans were not familiar spirits because they ate food, which *their* spirits did not. It is a clue, not just to the way Cook was perceived, but how his predecessors were, as the locals slowly realized that the newcomers did not fit their supernatural categories.

Cook and his crew sailed west and sighted the eastern coast of Australia – the first Europeans to do so – in April 1770. He had decided to sail home via the Dutch East Indies to get provisions and repairs. Having landed at Botany Bay, the journey continued, and then, on the night of 11 June, the *Endeavour* ran aground on the Great Barrier Reef. The mainland was 20 miles (30 km) away and there was a great deal of damage. About fifty tons of research material and other equipment had to be jettisoned overboard. By luck, the ship was eased off the reef the following day, and the hole in the hull was partially blocked by a large piece of coral. Cook beached the *Endeavour* to carry out urgent repairs near what is now the city of Cooktown. It was during this visit that he first saw crocodiles and kangaroos, and came to the conclusion that – although the people he met were some of the poorest on earth – they also seemed to be happy.

A map of Botany Bay in New South Wales, dated 1770 and probably drawn by Cook himself.

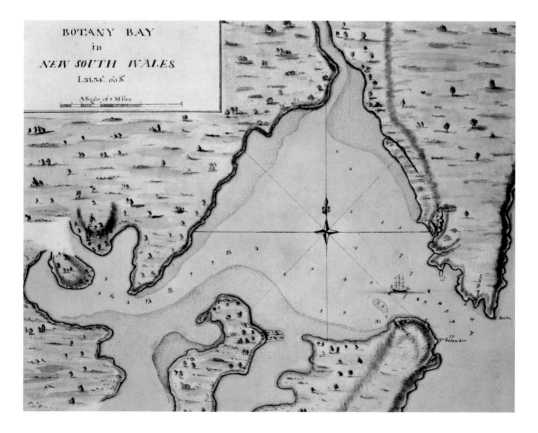

Arriving in the East Indies, Cook claimed New Zealand, New South Wales and the whole of the eastern coast of Australia for the British crown. But Batavia, modern-day Jakarta, turned out to be an unhealthy spot; seven of the crew died of dysentery, and so did Tupaia and his servant.

There is no doubt that the technology and techniques of exploration were much more sophisticated in Cook's time, compared to the exhausting voyage two and a half centuries before by Magellan. But the difficulties of understanding between the discoverers and the discovered were as great as ever. Cook, referring to the latter, complained to the diarist James Boswell over supper that 'their knowledge of the language was so imperfect that they required the aid of their senses, and any thing which they learnt about religion, government, or traditions might be quite erroneous.'[6]

The misunderstandings continued on Cook's next voyage, starting with a familiar encounter with cannibalism. This was a discovery made by the crew of Cook's deputy Tobias Furneaux, who was separated from Cook in the *Resolution* in an Antarctic fog, and had anchored alone in Queen Charlotte Sound. Furneaux sent ten men ashore to search for vegetables and they never came back. A search party found human remains, including a tattooed hand, apparently from a sailor, being eaten by dogs. The remains appeared to have been roasted.

When Cook went there himself later, he was determined to be forgiving, and to avoid the usual pattern whereby the new arrivals side with one or other of the local factions. 'If I had followed the advice of our pretended friends,' he wrote, 'I might have extirpated the whole race, for all the people of each hamlet or village, by turns, applied to me to destroy the others, a most striking proof of the divided state in which they live.' Cook managed to forgive Kahura, the chief believed to be responsible for the deaths, despite the revulsion of his crew. He even had his portrait painted.

Cook's second voyage made it into the Antarctic circle and finally laid to rest the myth of a huge southern continent. His third voyage was designed to find the Northwest Passage from the western end. But as this voyage progressed, the misunderstandings seemed to get worse: whether it was Cook's indisposition – despite his humane approach, he cut off the ears of a man who stole a sextant in Huahine,

A brass sextant of around 1770, supposedly once owned by Captain Cook.

one of the Society Islands – or whether it was the growing irritation of the islanders, the number of confrontations grew. There was nearly a disaster on Tonga during a feast with local chiefs, including the immense Fatafehi Paulaho, who Cook called 'an indolent, fat, greasy rogue', and who required two attendants to put food in his mouth for him.[7] It transpired later that there had been a plot to kill Cook and his officers over dinner, which was called off quite by chance.

Cook's second arrival in Hawaii in 1779 saw an unprecedented reception committee of over 1,500 canoes. The local chief, Palea, came on board with Koa, the high priest, and king Kalaniopuu followed. Cook gave him his own belt and sword. But it became clear that they were continuing in the great tradition of mistaking the newcomers for supernatural or semi-divine apparitions. Cook was apparently being identified with Lono, the local god of happiness and agriculture, whose festival was happening at the time.[8]

However, within a few days the crew of the *Resolution* seemed to be outstaying their welcome. Their hosts were tiring of them, and they were becoming expensive to supply. The priests were afraid that the presence of Lono himself was bound to diminish their power.

A view of 'Christmas Harbour' in the Kerguelen Islands in the southern Indian Ocean, from a selection of watercolours by John Webber, the official artist on Cook's last voyage.

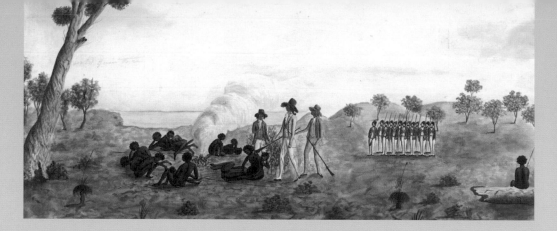

Trust and Distrust

The early pioneers tended to combine extremes of trust and distrust about the people they met. On the one hand, there was the basic human need to encounter the unexplained and unexpected and trust it, as Columbus did on Watling Island, delighted at the innocence of the people he had met. The case against trust was put by French explorer Marion du Fresne's lieutenant Julien Crozet, shocked by the murder of his captain: 'I contend that among all created animals there is nothing more savage and dangerous than the natural and savage, peoples themselves,' he wrote. 'I endeavoured to stimulate their curiosity, to learn the emotion that could be awakened in their souls, but found nothing but vicious tendencies among these children of nature; and they are all the more dangerous in that they greatly surpass Europeans in physical strength.'[9] This was the precise opposite of philosopher Jean-Jacques Rousseau's view of the noble savage,

A 1790 encounter between British colonists and Australian aborigines at Botany Bay.

which was even then inspiring a wave of revolutionary fervour across Europe. Yet somehow the two attitudes towards the people these Europeans encountered – innocence and fear – seemed to be two sides of the same experience.

Cook had their tents and observatory brought back aboard, and he sailed on 4 February. There were affectionate farewells.

Six days later, after the foremast was damaged, they were back. The Hawaiian locals were not pleased. They were even less pleased when one of them was given 140 lashes for theft. When some of the armourer's tools were stolen, Cook's shore party was forced to abandon their boat and swim out of the harbour to safety. When the ship's large cutter was stolen, Cook ordered that Kalaniopuu should be taken as a hostage until it was returned. The king agreed, but when he reached the shore one of his wives rushed up weeping, begging him not to go. There were, by now, about 2,000 people watching the melee and Cook had his marines drawn up along the beach. It was then that news spread through the crowd that one of the chiefs had been shot.

Events got rapidly out of hand. A furious man ran up to Cook brandishing a spear. Whether he lost his temper or was genuinely fearful for his life, Cook shot him and the fighting was soon general. Determined that their withdrawal should be dignified, Cook turned to wave to the boats to come into the beach to pick up his party. It was at this point that he was felled by a blow to the back of the head, probably from the high priest, Koa. He disappeared from view, and dozens of men leapt on top of him and stabbed him in the shallow water. The crew arrived back on board on tears. 'A general silence ensued throughout the ship,' wrote one of the sailors, 'it appearing to us somewhat like a dream that we could not reconcile ourselves to for some time.'[10]

A wooden spear from Hawaii, like those brandished against Cook on his final visit.

After his death, we all wailed. His bones were separated – the flesh was seared off and burnt, as was the practice in regard to our own chiefs when they died.

Perspective on Cook's death from a Hawaiian native[11]

On board the *Resolution*, ship's master William Bligh – soon to be famous for inspiring the mutiny on the *Bounty* – argued for terrible revenge. Cook's deputy Charles Clerke managed to persuade the crew to wait while they collected the bodies and scientific equipment. As if on cue, Koa swam out to the ship with a white flag of peace, and promised to bring Cook's remains back. A scalp which appeared to have been Cook's was delivered later. The danger that Cook's legacy would be as brutal as his predecessors seemed to have been averted.

Cook had disproved the existence of the southern continent and, although he had failed to quite disprove the reality of a Northwest Passage, he believed its existence to be very unlikely. When the Arctic explorer Robert McClure did find it in 1853, with his starving expedition going insane around him, he realized it would be impassable to commercial shipping. Cook's death unleashed a huge wave of exploration, mainly searching for botanical specimens, by the English, French and Spanish. William Bligh set forth in the *Bounty* to collect breadfruit trees. One of Cook's midshipmen, George Vancouver, set up base camp on Nootka Sound on the American Pacific coast and headed inland. From Lewis and Clark in the United States to David Livingstone in Africa, from Charles Francis Hall in the North Pole to Robert Falcon Scott in the South, there was still a great deal to explore and more to encounter.

Cook's part in his own death has been debated ever since. In 2004, the earliest depiction of the events, by John Cleveley the Younger, the brother of the ship's carpenter, finally came to light having been lost for a century and a half. It was painted in 1784 and shows Cook brandishing a musket – a more violent scene than that shown in traditional paintings.[12] But there is no doubt that his crew were devastated by the loss. Cook's surgeon's mate paid tribute to him, writing 'In every situation, he stood unrivalled and alone: on him all eyes were turned: he was our leading star, which at its setting left us involved in darkness and despair.'[13]

Cook's genius was in his curiosity and his constant efforts to understand accurately what he was seeing with European eyes. Other pioneers had taken part in local ceremonies in a halting attempt to communicate, but Cook really immersed himself in the possibilities of knowledge, despite his taciturn and distant exterior. He made detailed notes about everything, from fishing nets to weaving cloth out of bark, and was constantly frustrated by the failure of those he met to learn from the newcomers. He was thrilled when the chief in Tonga suddenly asked them why they were there. It was a glimpse of curiosity like his own.

Transplanting breadfruit trees from Tahiti in 1796: Cook's master William Bligh was sent to collect them in the South Seas on his own disastrous voyage.

One of his lieutenants caught sight of him in Tonga taking part in the chief's procession, naked to the waist with his hair hanging down. 'I do not pretend to dispute the propriety of Capn Cook's conduct,' wrote the disapproving officer, 'but I cannot help thinking he rather let himself down.'[14]

It is tempting to believe that Cook managed to turn a page in the history of exploration and, in a way, he did. But the next page seemed depressingly like the last when it came to the often fatal encounters between explorers and explored. Three years after Cook's visit to New Zealand, a French expedition under Marion du Fresne massacred 250 Māoris after their commander was killed. In 1793, the lieutenant governor of Norfolk Island (discovered by Cook in 1774) had two Māoris kidnapped just to explain how their flax industry worked. And in the following century, the genocide of the original inhabitants of Tasmania cast a terrible shadow over the settlement of Australia. Still to come were the horrors of the exploitation of the Congo, and all the other 20th-century cruelties and destruction, which carry on to this day in the name of logging or beef or rubber or minerals. The history of these encounters between worlds is still not finished.

The earliest portrayal of Cook's death, showing him brandishing a musket. It was painted by John Cleveley the Younger, the brother of a crew member who had sketched the scene on the spot.

Conclusion: The Impact of the Encounters

Most of the initial encounters outlined in this book tended towards a bloody conclusion, if not immediately then in the fullness of time. Some of the pioneering Europeans in this book were gentler than others – as presumably were some of those they encountered – but, time after time, the strange meetings led to immediate violence or long-term cruelty or both. Even James Cook, one of the most humane explorers, was destined to lose his life in an unexpectedly violent encounter on a beach in Hawaii.

There were any number of miscategorizations and misunderstandings between the explorers and the explored which led to these outcomes. What is fascinating are the exceptions – the relationship between Cook and Tupaia or perhaps even between Cortés and Moctezuma which, despite everything, became cordial and almost fond. There is also evidence of human care, not just by the sophisticated Europeans for bewildered locals, but for bewildered explorers by the people they encountered.

When five of Martin Frobisher's crewmen went missing, for example, they were believed to have been lost, murdered and possibly even eaten for three centuries until an American explorer stumbled over the remains of Frobisher's camp while he was searching for Sir John Franklin's ill-fated Arctic expedition. For the first time, he listened in detail to the tales of the Inuit he met, and noted down what they said. He came to believe that Frobisher's men had lived on among the Inuit, cared for by them. In the same way, the first Australian colonists in Botany Bay relied heavily on help from the

An encounter between two worlds: a sketch by ship's artist John Webber of Captain Cook presenting a medal to an aborigine in Adventure Bay, Tasmania, 29 January 1777. Medals and other trinkets were among the gifts distributed by Cook.

Cartier's encounter in Canada, depicted on a 16th-century map; it was almost an exception to the iron rule of bloody encounters.

people who lived nearby, just as the inhabitants of Jamestown relied on support and instruction from the Native Americans.

One of the strangest tales is one involving Amerigo Vespucci, who was unwittingly to give his name to the New World, and his encounter with the 'giants' of the island of Curaçao. He and his party were enjoying a meal made by the women in the village they had found, discussing how to kidnap two daughters and take them back to Spain. Suddenly, there were voices outside, and a large number of tall, well-armed men arrived back from hunting. The visitors were questioned using sign language. Where were they from? What did they want? Vespucci replied that they were travelling around the world and came in peace. The idea of kidnapping the two girls was dropped, and the men escorted them politely and firmly back to their boats. It was one of those encounters which could have ended in disaster but actually ended in dignity and mutual respect.

Another exception is the story of the French navigator Jacques Cartier, who was sailing up the St Lawrence River in 1535 to the Huron-Iroquois settlement on the site of what is now Quebec, the winter home of the tribe. A French landing party encountered a group of these Native Americans, who were terrified by their strange faces and clothes and were about to run away. But with the newcomers were the two sons of their chief, who Cartier had negotiated to take back to France after his first voyage. Taignoagny and Domagaya called after them in their own language. Recognizing them despite their French costume, there was a huge welcome and great deal of leaping and shouting, and soon canoes were arriving with corn and pumpkins from the fields. There was a solemn ceremony beside the ships, while Cartier's sailors handed out food and wine.

Human nature is so paradoxical that, inevitably, some of the encounters were enthusiastic and open-handed. But even these were hard to sustain. Columbus's joyful meetings on Watling Island were followed by the horrors of the *encomienda*. Vespucci did his share of seizing locals and was, in any case, a seasoned slave trader. Even Cartier's happy reunion ended, without him fully understanding why, in mistrust. Taignoagny and Domagaya were sullen about his intention to carry on up river, and, despite continued good relations, Cartier was uncomfortably aware that he was listening to local war cries. Later historians speculated that, despite Cartier's fears, the locals had no violent intentions towards them. It was just that they believed Cartier's expedition was supernatural, with their ability to somehow float on the water, and they didn't want to lose them, and certainly not to rival tribes.

Those who wrote about these encounters in the generations that followed were satisfied that the explorers were often categorized initially as supernatural beings, but we have to realize the limits to what we know. There is a dividing line in the academic debate, which crystallizes around the arguments of anthropologists like the American iconoclast Marshall Sahlins, who argued that the natives of Hawaii and the rest of the Pacific had a completely different understanding from Cook and his predecessors. On the other side are those in the camp of his Sri Lankan colleague Gananath Obeyesekere, whose interpretation of Cook's demise is that, actually, however primitive indigenous societies might seem, they still thought much the same as westerners.[1]

It is true that many breakdowns in amicable relations between newcomers and locals – especially in the Pacific – were also because

A young man killed while trying to make contact with Indian women, from a German translation of the Soderini letter, a forgery purporting to be by Amerigo Vespucci.

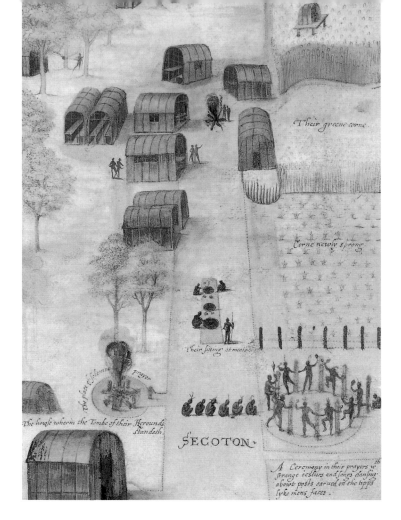

The Algonquin village of Secoton on the Carolina coast, drawn in the 1580s by John White, the first Englishman to record the inhabitants of the New World.

the pioneers outstayed their welcome. They particularly tested the ability of their hosts to continue supplying them, and the usual sullen, apparently inexplicable shifts in mood and deepening suspicion characterized the encounters.

Sahlins relates the tale of the whaler William Cary, marooned in Fiji in the 1820s, and questioned closely by a local chief. 'Are you a spirit?' he was asked.

No, said Cary, he was flesh and blood.

'Well,' said the chief. 'If you are the same as me, what makes you so white?'[2]

It is unclear, even if those indigenous communities believed the newcomers were somehow supernatural, exactly what they meant by that. Did they just mean 'foreign'? Did that make communication impossible? But even the Europeans fell back on theological categories to explain the people they encountered, whether they were pagan or heathen, Christian or Muslim.

One of the other perplexing aspects of these encounters is how little the two sides managed to learn from each other, apart from to distrust very quickly. Even the humane Cartier was influenced by the stories of massacres he had heard. It would be hard not to be, and these encounters did not tend to last long enough for the two sides to learn to trust each other, even if any basis for trust had been there. Often no trust was possible because the purpose of the visit made it impossible. While Columbus was awed by the innocence of the Taínos, he was at the same time writing back to Queen Isabella about their malleability. 'They are yours to command and make them work, sow seed and do whatever else is necessary,' he said, 'and build a town and teach them to wear clothes and adopt our customs.'[3]

There were also moments of amazement at the sophistication of the cultures the pioneers encountered. Vasco da Gama's arrival in Calicut harbour, for example, with its hundreds of ships, traders and races from all over the East. Or Cortés, arm in arm with Moctezuma, gazing down on the huge city of Tenochtitlan with its untold wealth. Or the astonished European colonists in the American northeast in the 16th century, confronted with Algonquin villages and miles and miles of open fields and sophisticated agriculture.

Many of the people the Europeans encountered were confused by the priorities of the new arrivals, particularly their obsession with gold. Some of Moctezuma's men assumed that the Europeans must eat it. In fact, the fixation on gold and financial profit blinded the newcomers to the value of what they found in the New World. They saw a land that could be exploited only in terms of plantations or extraction. It was always an unequal encounter, where the charm of the indigenous peoples gave way to irritation that they were not faster at producing gold. Columbus believed they were ignorant about the real value of things, and wrote about the 'trifles' he exchanged with them. In fact, he was deluding himself: he knew far too little about what the locals valued and why.

Aztec craftsmen smelting gold, from the Florentine Codex, a collection of Aztec documents.

OPPOSITE An illustration
from the 1552 *Book of
Medicinal Plants of the
Indians*, showing a plant
from the acacia family
(centre) and brazilwood
(left). The roots are drawn
around a glyph probably
representing 'soil'.

This was a serious mistake, even in terms of exploration. The failure of the early settlements in the New World, and the struggles of those that survived, demonstrated just how much the settlers were failing to understand about local agriculture. Plant breeding was more sophisticated than in Europe at this time. There was a better understanding of practical obstetrics and pharmacology. We have only recently come to understand the pharmacological possibilities hidden in the rainforests which are now disappearing day by day. Native Americans further north were taller than their European counterparts, had a better diet and were healthier. They had as much to teach as they had to learn.

The Curse of Gold

Gold and silver emerged from the New World in huge amounts, and the Spanish used this influx of money to buy the spices, silks and Eastern luxuries they craved, as well as the products they used to make and grow in Spain. The precious metals began to filter through intricate networks of merchants out to India and China. They also filtered north, partly because of the activities of pirates who preyed on the Spanish convoys, and partly because of the consumption of dried cod in southern Europe. The long-term effect on the Spanish economy was debilitating inflation, which seriously weakened their empire. The English had hoped for spices from Cabot's voyages, but when instead they found a huge weight of cod off the Newfoundland coast, they temporarily gave up the whole idea of serious exploration. In fact, by the end of the 16th century, cod were being hauled out of the Atlantic at the rate of 200 million a year. Ironically, the cod caught there began to earn the gold and silver that the Spanish were mining and transporting so laboriously from the New World.

Aztec gold: the Spanish melted down vast quantities of New World goldwork into bullion so surviving pieces like this are rare.

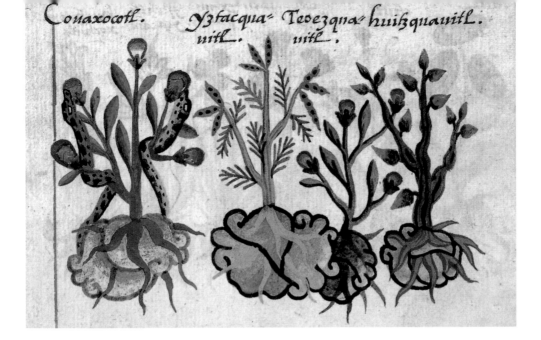

Conaxocotl. Yztacquauitl. Teoezquauitl. huitzquauitl.

On the other hand, Cook was continually frustrated at the failure of the people he met to learn from him. He was excited at any evidence of wider curiosity, like Tupaia's. They certainly learned techniques and eventually habits from the Europeans who arrived so unexpectedly. But once the relationships had settled down from the first astonished speculation to something longer term, they were often less than impressed. The Taínos were astonished by the cruelty of the Europeans, at least according to Spanish priest Bartolomé de las Casas, and other tribes were amazed at their occasional incompetence. They floundered around in the forests of North America, or the Arctic ice, apparently unable to help themselves, dressed in bizarre or inadequate clothing, either far too hot or far too cold. But they were impressed by the power of the Europeans, their technology and weaponry, and – in the New World at least – by their horses. When a chief begged Cartier to fire his cannons, because he heard they made an impressive sound, the echoing explosions fired into the forests caused many of the locals to panic.

Over a longer period of time, although the two sides may not have learned enough from each other, the exchanges in biodiversity ushered in by Columbus and Cabot and those that followed had a

Bartolomé de las Casas, one of the great humanitarian campaigners of the New World.

OPPOSITE The first printed representation of maize in Europe, published in Basel, Switzerland, in 1542.

Two afflicted women praying to the Virgin, and a corpse covered with syphilitic eruptions: syphilis was one of the first of the Columbian exchanges.

huge effect on humanity. The descendants of the few horses and cattle transported to the New World in the holds of Columbus's ships on his second voyage spread out across the American continent in the centuries that followed. Within a century, huge wild packs of them were heading north, and providing a whole new means of transport for the Native Americans, expanding their horizons and possibilities. In exchange, the Europeans got cochineal after the conquistadors came across Aztecs selling it in the marketplaces of Mexico in 1519. This dye, derived from a small insect, was so powerful and brilliant that it overshadowed all the other colours. When German peasants rose in revolt in 1526, one of their demands was the right to wear red.

What was difficult to predict were the economic effects of these encounters in the centuries that followed. The Native American appetite for European metal goods began to grow, and the beaver pelts they exchanged were farmed more intensely as a result, driving beavers close to extinction, and taking time away from agriculture – which meant they had to trade with other tribes further south for a greater proportion of their food. The same story was repeated in different ways all over the globe.

It was not until 1586 that Francis Drake seized a cargo of potatoes from a Spanish ship from America, and brought them to Europe, where they quickly became a staple diet of the poor. There are other stories that the first potatoes arrived in Ireland, the first nation to embrace them as a food, washed ashore from the Armada two years later. With potatoes came pumpkins, squash, peanuts, tomatoes, avocados, tobacco, papayas, mahogany, rubber, cocoa and maize. Maize was an Arawak word meaning the 'stuff of life'. Like potatoes, maize took a roundabout route to Europe, seized by Barbary pirates preying on Spanish shipping and taken to Turkey, which meant it was known originally as 'turkey wheat'. Tobacco, chocolate and cocaine came the same way. Going the other way were wheat, barley, almonds, mulberries, cherries, walnuts, apples, indigo, oranges, lemons, grapefruit and rice.

More devastating were the diseases. Columbus and his men are believed to have been the source of the fearsome outbreak of syphilis in Europe, when it emerged among French troops outside Naples in 1494. Within a generation, one writer was estimating that it had

TVRCICVM
FRVMENTVM.
Türckisch korn.
Turkish wheat.

affected one million people in Europe and it had already made its way all the way round the globe to China. It is tempting to suspect that some of the mysterious early deaths of mariners – John Cabot, for example, and Columbus's difficult deputy Martin Alonso Pinzón – may have been the result of syphilis.

But the germs which went the other way in the Columbian exchange were even more destructive. Nearly the whole population of the Antilles died in 1493 after Columbus's arrival. Flu and smallpox spread through the Aztec and Inca empires, facilitating the victory of the conquistadors. Centuries later, Europeans visiting the forests of North America described the dead lying all over.

The extraordinary ability of germs and diseases to circulate around the world gives a clue to the meaning of these encounters. Human beings might not always be able to handle their unexpected encounters with each other with trust and generosity, but we should not pretend that they were completely alien to each other. The human race spread across the globe from common beginnings, so their encounters were never entirely new. Their expressions and their gestures were capable of being understood, even if that understanding was prone to confusion. In many cases, the human encounters were simply the inevitable result of other kinds of exploration. Their germs and diseases had often gone before them, and so had their goods and their precious metals to pay for them. Silks, spices and dyes had been travelling from East to West for centuries before Vasco da Gama or Magellan followed in person. The idea that these encounters were somehow the forerunners of modern globalization is, in that sense, quite wrong.

There was something unique, though, about the voyages of discovery. From the moment Columbus set foot in the New World to the moment when Magellan's depleted crew found they had travelled all the way round the world, a dramatic phase of human history was unfolding. It was a period of shock for both sides, for explorers and explored, to see themselves in a mirror – even if they had no concept of such a thing – perhaps for the first time. We have never quite recovered, and the abuses and the forced trade continue even now, but it does at least tell us something about our humanity.

OPPOSITE A 19th-century encounter: a wooden leg was made by Arctic explorer John Ross's carpenter in return for Inuit help when his expedition was marooned on the ice for four years.

Resources

Chronology

1421 Chinese Admiral Zheng He sets out on a voyage which probably reached Africa

1450 Prince Henry 'the Navigator' creates an institute for exploration at Sagres in Portugal

1453 The fall of Constantinople cuts off trade routes from East to West

1487 Bartholomew Dias discovers the Cape of Good Hope

1492 Christopher Columbus embarks on his first voyage to the New World

1493 John Cabot probably sees Columbus in Valencia

1494 The Treaty of Tordesillas divides the world between Castile and Portugal

1497 John Cabot discovers his 'New Founde Land'

1498 Cabot sets out on his second voyage and disappears from history

Vasco da Gama reaches India

Columbus's third voyage sights the American mainland for the first time

1500 Pedro Alvares Cabral claims Brazil for the Portuguese

Gaspar Corte Real sails from Lisbon for the far north

1501 Amerigo Vespucci travels south down the Latin American coast with a Portuguese expedition

1506 Columbus dies in Valladolid

1507 Martin Waldseemüller publishes the first world map to use the word 'America'

1509 Lopes de Sequira reaches Malacca for the Portuguese

1510 Afonso de Albuquerque takes Goa

1513 Vasco Núñez de Balboa sees the Pacific

1517 First trading links between China and the Portuguese

1519 Ferdinand Magellan sets out to reach the East via a Southwest Passage

1521 Hernán Cortés storms the Aztec empire

Magellan is killed in the Philippines

1522 The survivors of Magellan's expedition return to Castile, having circumnavigated the world

1524 Giovanni da Verrazzano sails along the North American coast for the French

1526 Sebastian Cabot explores the River Plate

1533 Francisco Pizarro overwhelms the Inca empire

1534 Jacques Cartier discovers the St Lawrence River

1576 Martin Frobisher searches for the Northwest Passage

1580 Francis Drake becomes the first English captain to circumnavigate the world

1642 Abel Tasman sights Tasmania and New Zealand

1766 Louis de Bougainville sets out on his circumnavigation of the world

1768 James Cook sets out on his first voyage

1779 Cook is killed during a dispute with Hawaiian islanders

1820 A Russian expedition is the first to sight Antarctica

1845 John Franklin arrives in the Arctic on his ill-fated expedition to find the Northwest Passage

Notes

Introduction

1 Eber, D.H. (2008), *Encounters on the Passage*, University of Toronto Press.
2 Quoted in Fernandez-Armesto (2007).
3 Fairbank, J.K., E.O. Reischauer & A.M. Craig (1965), *East Asia: The Modern Transformation*, Vol. 2 of *A History of East Asian Civilization*, London: George Allen & Unwin, 77.
4 Merrell, J.H. (2000), 'The Indian's New World: The Catawba Experience' in P.C. Mancall & J.H. Merrell (eds.), *American Encounters: Natives and Newcomers From European Contact to Indian Removal 1500–1850*, New York: Routledge.
5 Quoted in D. Abulafia (2008), *The Discovery of Mankind: Atlantic Encounters in the Age of Columbus*, New Haven: Yale University Press.
6 Merrell (2000), op. cit.

Chapter 1

1 Quoted in C.R. Beazley (1894), *Prince Henry the Navigator*, London: Putnam.
2 Subrahmanyam (1997), 98.
3 Thatcher, O.J. (ed.) (1907), *The Library of Original Sources*, Vol. V: 9th to 16th Centuries, Milwaukee: University Research Extension Co.
4 Subrahmanyam, S. (1990), *The Political Economy of Commerce: Southern India 1500–1650*, Cambridge University Press, 7.
5 Velho (1995), 54–55.
6 Ravenstein, E.G. (1898), *A Journal of the First Voyage of Vasco da Gama, 1497–1499*, London: Hakluyt Society, 131.
7 Steensgaard, N. (1974), *The Asian Trade Revolution of the Seventeenth Century*, University of Chicago Press, 407.

Chapter 2

1 Morison, S.E. (1942) *Admiral of the Ocean Sea*, Oxford University Press, 223.
2 Ibid., 229.
3 Wilson, I. (1991), *The Columbus Myth*, London: Simon & Schuster, 77.
4 Morison (1942), op. cit., 231.

5 Quinn, D. (1998), *European Approaches to North America, 1450–1640*, Aldershot: Ashgate, 32–33.
6 Fernandez-Armesto, F. (1974), *Columbus and the Conquest of the Impossible*, London: Weidenfeld & Nicolson, 97.
7 Fernandez-Armesto, F. (1992) *Columbus on Himself*, London: Folio Society, 158.

Chapter 3

1 Williamson (1962), 84.
2 Jones, E. (2007), 'Alwyn Ruddock: John Cabot and the Discovery of America', *Historical Research* 81/212:224–254.
3 Quoted in Williamson (1962), 216.
4 Quoted in Vaughan, A.T. (2006), *Transatlantic Encounters: American Indians in Britain 1500–1776*, Cambridge University Press.
5 Eber (2008), op. cit., 4.

Chapter 4

1 Quoted in Masini, G. (1998), *How Florence Invented America*, New York: Marsilio Publishers, 36.
2 Pigafetta, A. (2010), *First Voyage Round the World by Magellan: Translated From the Accounts of Pigafetta and Other Contemporary Writers*, ed. H. Stanley, Cambridge University Press, 50.
3 Ibid., 69.
4 Pigafetta (1966), 121.
5 Quoted in Estensen, M. (2006), T*erra Australis Incognita: The Spanish Quest for the Mysterious Great South Land*, Sydney: Allen & Unwin, 15.

Chapter 5

1 Collis, M. (1954), *Cortés and Montezuma*, London: Faber & Faber, 123.
2 Ibid., 123–24.
3 Quoted in Wood, M. (2000), *Conquistadors*, London: BBC Books, 70–71.
4 Kirkpatrick (1988), 98.
5 Xeres, F. (1874), *Reports on the Discovery of Peru*, ed. and trans. C. Markham, New York: Burt Franklin Publishers, 1.

Chapter 6

1 James Cook's Journal, 22 April 1770, National Library of Australia.
2 Beaglehole (1961).
3 James Cook's Journal, 16 May 1768, National Library of Australia.
4 Morison, S.E. (ed.) (1963), *Journals and Other Documents on the Life and Voyages of Christopher Columbus*, New York: Heritage, 227.
5 Salmond, A. (1991), *Two Worlds: First Meetings Between Maori and Europeans 1642–1772*, Honolulu: University of Hawaii Press, 87–88.
6 Quoted in O'Sullivan, D. (2008), *In Search of Captain Cook*, London: J.B. Tauris, 127.
7 Ibid., 158.
8 This is doubted by Obeyesekere (1992).
9 Moorehead, A. (1966), *The Fatal Impact: An Account of the Invasion of the South Pacific 1767–1840*, London: Hamish Hamilton.
10 Able Seaman George Gilbert, quoted in Hough, R. (1979), *The Murder of Captain James Cook*, Basingstoke: Macmillan, 229.
11 Quoted in Ellis, W. (1826), *Narrative of a Tour Through Hawaii*, London: Fisher, 117.
12 Stevenson, A. (2004), 'Captain Cranky, Portrait of an Old Explorer Behaving Badly', *Sydney Morning Herald*, July 14.
13 Kippis, A. (1820), *Narrative of the Voyages Round the World, Performed by Captain James Cook*, Chiswick: Whittingham.
14 Beaglehole (1967), 151.

Conclusion

1 Obeyesekere (1992).
2 Sahlins (1994), 75.
3 Fernandez-Armesto (1974), op. cit., 97.

Further Reading

Beaglehole, J.C. (ed.) (1961–67), *The Journals of Captain James Cook*, Cambridge University Press.

Boyle, D. (2008), *Toward the Setting Sun: Columbus, Cabot and Vespucci and the Race for America*, New York: Walker Books.

Fernandez-Armesto, F. (2007), *Pathfinders: A Global History of Exploration*, Oxford University Press.

Kirkpatrick, F.A. (1988), *The Spanish Conquistadores*, London: Century Hutchinson.

Macgillivray, A. (2006), *A Short History of Globalization*, London: Constable & Robinson.

Morison, S.E. (1971), *The European Discovery of America: The Northern Voyages AD 500–1600*, New York: Oxford University Press.

Morison, S.E. (1974), *The European Discovery of America: The Southern Voyages AD 1492–1616*, New York: Oxford University Press.

Obeyesekere, G. (1992), *The Apotheosis of Captain Cook*, Princeton University Press.

Pigafetta, A. (1966), *First Around the World: A Journal of Magellan's Voyage*, trans. J.A. Robertson, London: Hamish Hamilton.

Sahlins, M. (1994), 'The discovery of the true savage', in D. Merwick (ed.), *Essays in Honour of Greg Dening*, Parkville: University of Melbourne.

Subrahmanyam, S. (1997), *The Career and Legend of Vasco da Gama*, Cambridge University Press.

Velho, A. (1995), *A Journal of the First Voyage of Vasco da Gama*, trans. E.G. Ravenstein, New Delhi: Asian Educational Services.

Williamson, J.A. (1962), *The Cabot Voyages and Bristol Discovery under Henry VII*, Cambridge University Press.

Translations and Transcriptions of the Documents

1 The Santa Fe Capitulations, the agreement between Columbus and Isabella of Castile, set down in April 1492, which promised him huge rewards. The Castilian negotiators believed that, if Columbus really did find a western route to the Indies, these rewards would be worth paying. The relevant text ends near the top of the right-hand page.

The things requested and that Your Highnesses give and grant to Sir Christopher Columbus in partial reward for what he has discovered in the Ocean Seas and will discover on the voyage that now, with the help of God, he is to make on the same seas in the service of Your Highnesses, are the following:

First, Your Highnesses, as the lords you are of the Ocean Seas, appoint Sir Christopher Columbus from now on as your admiral on all those islands and mainland discovered or acquired by his command and expertise in the Ocean Seas during his lifetime and, after his death, by his heirs and successors one after the other in perpetuity, with privileges and prerogatives equal to those that Sir Alfonso Enríquez, your high admiral of Castile, and his other predecessors in the office held in their districts. It pleases Their Highnesses. Juan de Coloma.

Also, Your Highnesses appoint Sir Christopher your viceroy and governor general in all those islands and any mainland and islands that he may discover and acquire in the seas. For the governance of each and every one of them, he will nominate three persons for each office, and Your Highnesses will select and appoint the one most beneficial to your service, and thus the lands that our Lord permits him to find and acquire will be best governed to the service of Your Highnesses. It pleases Their Highnesses. Juan de Coloma.

You wish him to have and take for himself one-tenth of all and any merchandise, whether pearls, precious stones, gold, silver, spices, and any other things and merchandise of whatever kind, name,

or sort it may be, that is bought, exchanged, found, acquired, and obtained within the limits of the admiralty that Your Highnesses from now on bestow on Sir Christopher, deducting all the relevant expenses incurred, so that, of what remains clear and free, he may take and keep one-tenth for himself and do with it as he pleases, reserving the other nine-tenths for Your Highnesses. It pleases Their Highnesses. Juan de Coloma.

Should any lawsuits arise on account of the merchandise that he brings back from the islands and mainland acquired or discovered, or over merchandise taken in exchange from other merchants there in the place where this commerce and trade is held and done, and if taking cognizance of such suits belongs to him by virtue of the privileges pertaining to his office of admiral, may it please Your Highnesses that he or his deputy, and no other judge, shall be authorized to take cognizance of and give judgment on it from now on. It pleases Their Highnesses, if it pertains to the office of admiral and conforms to what the admiral Sir Alfonso Enríquez and his other predecessors had in their districts, and if it be just. Juan de Coloma.

On all vessels outfitted for trade and business, each time, whenever, and as often as they are outfitted, Sir Christopher Columbus, if he wishes, may contribute and pay one-eighth of all that is spent on the outfitting and likewise he may have and take one-eighth of the profits that result from such outfitting. It pleases Their Highnesses. Juan de Coloma.

These are authorized and dispatched with the replies from Your Highnesses at the end of each article. In the town of Santa Fe de La Vega de Granada, on the seventeenth day of April in the year of the birth of our saviour Jesus Christ one thousand four hundred and ninety-two.

I, the King   I, the Queen
By command of the king and queen
Juan de Coloma

2 An early copy (the original is lost) of the letter that Columbus wrote to Luis de Santangel, Isabella of Castille's keeper of the privy purse, and the man who persuaded her to back Columbus's Indies voyage. It was written at sea during the return trip in February 1493 and describes Columbus's first impressions of the new world.

Sir: Since I know that you will be pleased by the great victory which Our Lord has given me on my voyage, I am writing you this letter, from which you will learn how in twenty days I crossed to the Indies with the fleet which the King and Queen, our most illustrious sovereigns, gave me. I found there very many islands inhabited by people without number, and I have taken possession of them all on behalf of Their Highnesses by proclamation and by unfurling the royal standard, and I was not contradicted. To the first island I found I gave the name San Salvador in memory of His High Majesty who miraculously has given all this; the Indians call it Guanahaní. To the second I gave the name the island of Santa María de Concepción; to the third, Fernandina; to the fourth, Isabela; to the fifth, the island of Juana, and so on, to each a new name. When I reached Juana I followed the coast to the west and I found it to be so large that I thought it must be the mainland, the province of Cathay; and since I found no towns or villages on the coast except small settlements with whose inhabitants I could not speak because they all immediately fled, I continued on that course thinking that I could not fail to find great cities or towns. After many leagues, having seen that there was nothing new and that the coast was carrying me northwards, which was not the course I wished to take because winter was now drawing on and I proposed to make to the south, and as moreover the wind was carrying me forward, I decided to wait no longer and I turned round and made for a fine harbour. From there I sent two men inland to find out if there was a king or any great cities. They travelled for three days and found an infinite number of small villages and countless people, but no sign of authority; for which reason they returned. I understood well enough from some other Indians I had already taken that the whole of this coast was an island; and so I followed the coast one hundred and seven leagues to the east to where it ended. From that cape I sighted another island to the east, eighteen leagues distant, to which I then gave the name Española, and I went there and followed the north coast due east as I had done in Juana for a good hundred and eighty-eight leagues, in a straight line to the east as I had in Juana. That coast like all the others is very rocky, and this one is particularly so. There are many harbours on the sea coast beyond comparison with any I know in Christendom, and so many good, wide rivers that it is a marvel. The land is high and there are many sierras and high mountains beyond comparison with the island of Tenerife, all most beautiful and of a thousand different shapes and all accessible and covered in trees of a thousand kinds and so high that they seem to reach the sky; and I am told that they never lose their leaves as far as I can understand, for I saw that they were as green and as beautiful as they are in Spain in May, and some were in flower and some in fruit, and some at another stage according to their nature, and there where I travelled the nightingale and other birds of a thousand kinds were singing in November. There are six or eight kinds of palms which are a wonder to behold for their beautiful variety, as too with the other trees and fruits and plants. There are marvellous pine groves and broad meadows, and there is honey and there are many different kinds of birds and many varieties of fruit. In the interior there are many mines of metal and incalculable numbers of people. Española is a marvel; the sierras and the mountains and the plains and the fields and the land are so beautiful and rich for planting and sowing, for raising all kinds of cattle, for building towns and villages. The harbours are beyond the belief of anyone who has not seen them, and the many great rivers give good waters of which the majority bear gold. There are great differences between the trees and fruit and plants and those of Juana. On this island there are many spices and great mines of gold and other metals. All the people on this island and all the others I have found or have learned of go naked, men and women alike, just as their mothers bear them, although some women cover themselves in one place with a leaf from a plant or a cotton garment which they make for the purpose. They have no iron or steel or weapons, nor are they that way inclined, not because they are not well built and of fine bearing, but because they are amazingly timid. They have no other weapons than those made from canes cut when they are in seed, to the ends of which they fix a sharp stick; and they dare not use them, for many times I have happened to send two or three men ashore to some town to speak to them and a great number of them have come out, and as soon as they see the men coming they run off, parents not even waiting for children, and not because any harm has been done to any of them; on the contrary, everywhere I have been and have been able to speak to them I have given them some of everything I had, cloth and many other things, without receiving anything in exchange; but they are simply incurably timid.

3 The letters patent granted to John Cabot and his sons by the English king Henry VII in March 1496, the founding document of the British claims to North America. Cabot set out some months later but was forced to turn back. It was not until the following year that his ship, the *Matthew*, came upon his 'Land First Seen'. The document anticipates complaints from Castile by only giving Cabot rights over lands 'unknown to all Christians'.

For John Cabot and his Sons
The King, to all to whom, etc. Greeting: Be it known and made manifest that we have given and granted as by these presents we give and grant, for us and our heirs, to our well-beloved John Cabot, citizen of Venice, and to Lewis, Sebastian and Sancio, sons of

the said John, and to the heirs and deputies of them, and of any one of them, full and free authority, faculty and power to sail to all parts, regions and coasts of the eastern, western and northern sea, under our banners, flags and ensigns, with five ships or vessels of whatsoever burden and quality they may be, and with so many and with such mariners and men as they may wish to take with them in the said ships, at their own proper costs and charges, to find, discover and investigate whatsoever islands, countries, regions or provinces of heathens and infidels, in whatsoever part of the world placed, which before this time were unknown to all Christians. We have also granted to them and to any one of them, and have given licence to set up our aforesaid banners and ensigns in any town, city, castle, island or mainland whatsoever, newly found by them. And that the before-mentioned John and his sons or their heirs and deputies may conquer, occupy and possess whatsoever such towns, castles, cities and islands by them thus discovered that they may be able to conquer, occupy and possess, as our vassals and governors lieutenants and deputies therein, acquiring for us the dominion, title and jurisdiction of the same towns, castles, cities, islands and mainlands discovered; in such a way nevertheless that of all the fruits, profits, enoluments, commodities, gains and revenues accruing from this voyage, the said John and sons and their heirs and deputies shall be bounden and under obligation for every their voyage, as often as they shall arrive at our port of Bristol, at which they are bound and holden only to arrive, all necessary charges and expenses incurred by them having been deducted, to pay to us, either in goods or money, the fifth part of the whole capital gained, we giving and granting to them and their heirs and deputies, that they shall be free and exempt from all payment of customs on all and singular the goods and merchandise that they may bring back with them from those places newly discovered.

And further we have given and granted to them and to their heirs and deputies, that all mainlands, islands, towns, cities, castles and other places whatsoever discovered by them, however numerous they may happen to be, may not be frequented or visited by any other subjects of ours whatsoever without the licence of the aforesaid John and his sons and of their deputies, on pain of loss as well of the ships or vessels daring to sail to these places discovered, as of all goods whatsoever. Willing and strictly commanding all singular our subjects as well as by land as by sea, that they shall render good assistance to the aforesaid John and his sons and deputies, and that they shall give them all their favour and help as well in fitting out the ships or vessels as in buying stores and provisions with their money and in providing the other things which they must take with them on the said voyage. In witness whereof, etc. Witness ourself at Westminster on the fifth day of March.

By the King himself, etc.

4 An extract from the first edition of Antonio Pigafetta's journal of his voyage around the world with Magellan and Elcano. Pigafetta was a young Venetian scholar and one of only eighteen men who survived to return to Spain on the *Victoria* in 1522. His account was published three years later in Paris in French. Here, Magellan and his crews, starving and sick after their crossing of the Pacific, and having had a hostile reception in the Mariana Islands, have moved on to the Philippines. Magellan has cautiously landed on an uninhabited island next to one that is; the tribe from that island have sailed out to meet him, and gifts have been exchanged.

These people entered into very great familiarity and friendship with us, and made us understand several things in their language, and the names of some islands which we saw before us. The island in which they lived is called Zzuluan [Samar, in the Philippines], which is not very large. We took great pleasure with them, because they were very merry and conversable. * The captain, seeing that they

were well disposed, to do them more honour led them to his ship and showed them all his merchandise, namely cloves, cinnamon, pepper, walnut, ginger, mace, gold, and all that was in the ship. He also caused his artillery to fire several times, whereat they were much afraid, so that they tried to leap from the ship into the sea. And they made signs that the things which the captain had shown them grew in the places whither we were going. And when they wished to depart, they took leave of the captain and of us with good grace, promising to see us return. * The island where we were is called Humunu [Homonhon]. But because we found there two springs of very clear water we named it Aquade, that is, the water of good signs. Because in that island we found the first signs of gold. And you find there much white coral, and tall trees which bear fruits smaller than an almond, and they are like pines. There were also many palm trees both good and bad. * In that place are several neighbouring islands. Wherefore we called them the Archipelago of St Lazarus. Which region and archipelago are in ten degrees of latitude toward the Arctic Pole, and one hundred and sixty-one degrees of longitude from the line of demarcation.

* On Friday the twenty-second of March, the aforesaid people who had promised to return came about noon with two boats loaded with the said cochi [coconuts], sweet oranges, a jar of palm wine, and a cock, to give us to understand that there were fowls in their country, and we purchased all that they brought. * The lord of those people was old, and had his face painted, and he wore hanging from his ears golden rings which they call Schione, and the others wore many gold bracelets and armlets, with a linen kerchief on their head. And we lay eight days in that place, where the captain every day visited the sick men whom he had put ashore on the island to recover. And every day he gave them water from the said cocho fruit, which greatly refreshed them. * Near the said island, there is another where there are people who have holes in their ears so large that they can pass their arm through. These people,

called Caphri, are heathen and go naked, except that round their nature they wear a cloth made of the bark of trees. Howbeit some of the better clad wear cotton cloth, fringed with embroidery of silk done with a needle. * These people are brown, fat and painted, and they annoint themselves with coconut oil and with beneseed oil to protect themselves from the severity of the sun and the wind. They have very black hair hanging to the waist, and they wear small daggers and knives, and lances adorned with gold, and several other things. And their boats are like ours.

 * On Monday of Holy Week, the twenty-fifth of March and Feast of Our Lady, in the afternoon, as we were ready to sail thence, I went on board our ship to fish and, putting my feet on a yard to go down to the store room, my feet slipped from me because it had rained, and I fell into the sea without anyone seeing me. And being about to drown, by chance my left hand caught hold of the foot of the mainsail which was in the sea, and I held on to it and began to call out until someone came to help me and pick me up in the boat. I was succoured, not by merit, but by the mercy and grace of the fount of pity. * This same day we set course between west and southwest, and we passed through the midst of four small islands, namely Cenalo, Hinnangar, Ibusson, and Abarien [islands lying in the Surigao Strait].

* Figure of the Island of Good Signs. And of the four other islands Cenalo, Hinnangar, Ibusson, and Abarien.

The marginal text reads:

Of the people of the island of Zzuluan; The honour done by the captain to the people of Zzuluan; The people of Zzuluan take leave of the captain; Of the island of Humunu, and the water of good signs; The Archipelago of St Lazarus; The aforesaid people returned with gifts to the captain; Of the lord of the people of Humunu; Of the people called Caphri; Accoutrements of the Caphri; Antonio Pigafetta

thought to drown in the sea; Islands by which the captain passed.

5 The title page of the second report written by Hernán Cortés to the Emperor Charles V, describing events since 1519 and his arrival in the Yucatan. He also describes the wealth of the Aztecs, Moctezuma and the amazing city of Tenochtitlan, that he was eventually able to overwhelm with just a few hundred troops.

Sent to his Sacred Majesty, the Emperor of Our Realm, by the Captain-General of New Spain, called Don Fernando Cortes, in which he gives an account of the countries and innumerable provinces which he has discovered in Yucatan, from the year 1519 to the present time, and has subjected to the Crown of His Royal Majesty. He makes special relation of a very great, and very rich, province called Culua, in which there are many great cities, and marvellous edifices, having much commerce and wealth. Amongst these there is one more marvellous and richer than all the others, called Temixtitan [Tenochtitlan], which by marvellous art has been built on a great lake; of which city and province, a very great lord, called Moctezuma, is king; in which, things, frightful to be heard, were suffered by the Captain, and the Spaniards. He describes at length the vast dominion of the said Moctezuma, and its customs and ceremonies, and how he is served.

6 The first two pages from *The Fate of the Indians of the New World*, the letter sent in 1522 by the tireless campaigner Bartolomé de las Casas to the young Emperor Charles V, urging a new humanitarian approach to the colonized peoples of the New World, ending the system of *encomiendas* which gave colonists ownership of the people on the land. He also, fatefully, suggested here that their labour should be replaced by slaves brought over from Africa.

An Opinion of Bartolomé de las Casas

About the Indians
In all that concerns the remedy for the Indians of all the Indies and the manner to do so that they may become Christians and preserve their lives and liberty, and that the Spaniards may not end up destroying them, there is no other way or method or order except that your Majesty might incorporate them in the royal Crown as your vassals – which they are, abolishing all of the *encomiendas* established in all the Indies, and not granting one or another Indian to any Spaniard for *encomienda* – not as vassal, or in feud, or in any other manner, because, according to long and very certain experience, whatever way the Spaniards take, they will kill and destroy them [the Indigenous] out of their covetousness to possess gold and riches. And, therefore, [for Your Majesty] to do otherwise is contrary to the law of God, grave mortal sin, and of greatest prejudice to and destruction of Your Majesty's royal patrimony.

About the Habitation of the Spaniards
The settlement and habitation of the Spaniards in the Indies is very necessary, as much for the conversion and good order of the Indians as for the maintenance of the state and of the dominion of your Majesty and the kings of Castile in the Indies. This settlement and habitation of the Spaniards in those said kingdoms and lands can be done very well and sustained without *encomiendas* or service of Indians – as in all the other parts of the world, settlements were made without using Indians; moreover, one does not read in any scripture that those who went to settle in new lands might tyrannize and oppress the people found in them, and might use the inhabitants against their will – in prejudice and detriment to their liberty, their very lives, and their women and children – unless they [the settlers] were tyrants, and charlatans, and robbers as was Nembroth

who oppressed the people – just as, until today, has been and is being done in the Indies.

This then is the manner to support the said settlement and habitation of the Spaniards: Your Majesty ought to grant many privileges to such settlers – especially to farmers and hardworking and diligent laborers: giving them many and very large lands, waters, and woodlands – but not taking from the Indians what they have and might be necessary for their own fields and sustenance; also giving the settlers some cattle, sheep, oxen, carts, hoes, and plow shears, as well as exemptions for twenty years, and many other things that we wrote about in particular in the eighteenth remedy of those that we gave. Also give them as favors that the houses and the town, where they [the Spaniards] settle, might be built by the Indians – and that the said Indians might do this in place of the tributes that they must give Your Majesty; thus, the Indians would not pay any tribute for as much time as might seem just, reasonable, and not harmful in the judgment of the Audiencias, the bishop, and the religious, who in this matter have jurisdiction, in order that the Indians might be exempted and consoled.

In such a case, I affirm that in many parts of the Indies, with only the third of the tributes and benefits that a Christian now has and brings to the Indies, a pueblo of forty vecinos would be built that might have at least a hundred and twenty persons; and, in many parts, there will be persons who with the said third of what they bring could build two pueblos. And thus, Your Majesty will have the two parts, of course, of the profits that today you do not have; and in place of a Christian or settler who before – it must truly be said – would destroy and not settle; rather, in your Indies, Your Majesty will send and establish 120 and 200 settlers who truly will settle the land, and not be depopulators and destroyers of it. And this third is enough for two years of expenses for the said farmers and settlers, and, after the two years have passed, Your Majesty will have it all. And thus it seems quite clear how inestimably profitable this settlement will be to Your Majesty, and how you will be served by countless Indians and by great numbers of Christians – not as now when they destroy one another.

Your Majesty will be able to give favors for several years to some selected persons – fifty thousand maravedís to one, a hundred to another, more to others, and less to others, in order to help them settle the land until they establish themselves. And also order them to be loaned or pledged some black slaves for whom they ought to pay within three or four years – or as your royal will and favor might be, and in which you will receive many helps and favors. Although giving the monies is not very necessary for the said settlement because it will be done without it, yet we confess that giving it to them for some time will be beneficial and the said settlement will grow more. In the event that Your Majesty may do the said favor, [let it be that your officials pay the said monies—and these be not exchanged in the form of Indians, so that the Christians may not use the occasion to do them [the Indigenous] harms].

7 An extract from James Cook's diary on 13 April 1769, where he describes his arrival at Tahiti (to observe the passage of Venus), and the strict rules he sets out to govern the conduct of his crew there. This includes the instruction to treat the locals with 'all imaginable humanity', along with careful restrictions on trade.

Remarkable Occurences at Georges Island – Note, The way of reckoning the Day in Sea Journals is from Noon to Noon, but as the Most material transactions at this Island must happen in the Day time this method will be attended with ilconveniences in inserting the transactions of each Day; for this reason I shall during our stay at this Island but no longer reckon the day according to the civil account, that is to begin and end at midnight —

We had no sooner come to an Anchor in Royal Bay as before Mentioned than a great number of the natives in their canoes came off to the Ship and brought with them Cocoa-nuts &ca and these they seem'd to set a great Value upon – amongest those that came off to the Ship was an elderly Man whose Name was is Owhaa, him the Gentlemen that had been here before in the Dolphin knew and had often spoke of him as one that had been of service to them, this man, / together with some others / I took on board, / and made much of him thinking that he might on some occasion be of use to us — As our stay at this place was not likly to be very Short, I thought it very necessary that some order should be Observe'd in Trafficing with the Natives: that such Merchantdize as we had on board for that purpose might continue to bear a proper value, and not leave it to every ones own particular fancy, which could not fail to bring on confution and quarels between us and the Natives, and would infallible Lesen the Value of such Articles as we had to Traffic with: in d order to prevent this the following Rules were Orderd to be observed /. viz /

RULES to be observe'd by every person in or belonging to His Majestys Bark the Endevour, for the better establishing a regular and uniform Trade for Provisions &ca: with the inhabitants of Georges Island —

1st: To endeavour by every fair means to cultivate a friendship with the Natives and to treat them with all imaginable humanity —

2d: A proper person or persons will be appointed to trade with the Natives for all manner of Provisions, Fruit, and other productions of the earth; and no officer or Seaman or other person belonging to the Ship, excepting such as are so appointed, shall Trade or offer to Trade for any sort of Provisions, Fruit or other productions of the earth, unless they have my leave so to do —

3d: Every person employ'd a shore on any duty what soever is strictly to attend to the same, and if by neglect he looseth any of his Arms or working tools, or suffers them to be stole, the full Value thereof will be charge'd against his pay, according to the Custom of the Navy in such cases – and ^he shall recive such farther punishment as the nature of the offence may deserve —

4th: The same penalty will be inflicted upon every person who is found to imbezzle, trade or offer to trade with any part of the Ships ^Stores of what nature soever [unless they]

5th: No Sort of Iron, or any thing that is made of Iron, or any sort of Cloth or other usefull or necessary articles are to be given in exchange for any thing but provisions — J.C.

As soon as the Ship was properly secure'd, I went on Shore accompanied by Mr. Banks and the other gentlemen, with a party of Men under arms, we took along with us Owhaa who conducted us to the place where the Dolphin water'd, and made signs to us as well as we could understand that we might occupy that ground but it happen'd not to be fit for our purpose —

No one of the Natives made the least oppossission at our landing but came to us with all imaginable marks of friendship and submission – We afterwards made a circuit through the Woods, and then came on board – We did not find the inhabitants to be numerous and ^therefore at first imagined that several of them had fled from their habitations upon our arrival in the Bay ^*but Mr. Gore & some others who had been here before observ'd that a very great revolution must have happen'd – not near the number of inhabitants a great number of houses raiz'd, har[d]ly a vestage of some to be seen, particularly what was call'd the Queens. and not so much as a Hog or Fowl was to be seen – no very agreeable discovery to us of

^whose Ideas of plenty upon arrival at this Island / from the report of the Dolphin / was carried to the very highest pitch.

8 A copy of a map of South Sea islands made by Tupaia on board the *Endeavour* in 1769 made by James Cook, together with his rendering of Tupaia's remarks about ships which had visited there before. These remarks are difficult to translate and controversial among historians, but may refer to a visit by the Mendaña expedition in 1595 and, possibly, by the missing Spanish ship *San Lesmes* which disappeared after passing through the Magellan Straits in 1526.

9 The chart of the South Pole and Southern Hemisphere drawn by James Cook and published in London on his return from his second voyage in 1777. Australia is clearly marked as 'New Holland'. It also pays tribute to his forerunners by marking the routes of some of the distinguished navigators that went before him.

Sources of Translations: **1** Nader, H. & L. Formisano (1996), *The Book of Privileges*, Vol II, UCLA Press; **2** Courtesy Professor Barry Ife (full text is available, as of 30 January 2011, at: http://www.ems.kcl.ac.uk/content/etext/e022.html); **3** Biggar, H.B. (ed.) (1911), *The Precursors of Jacques Cartier, 1497–1534*, Ottawa: Government Printing Bureau, 8–10; **4** Pigafetta, A. (1969), *Magellan's Voyage: A Narrative Account of the First Circumnavigation*, Vol. I, trans. R.A. Skelton. Yale University Press, 64–5; **5** MacNutt, F.A. (1908), *Fernando Cortes: His Five Letters of Relation to the Emperor Charles V*. Cleveland: Arthur H. Clark; **6** Courtesy David Orique, O.P. (full text is available, as of 30 January 2011, at: http://lccn.loc.gov/2007574376).

Sources of Illustrations

a = above, b = below, c = centre

Album/Oronoz/akg-images **26, 59**; British Library/akg-images **34, 102, 120, 121**; Marc Charmet/Private Collection/The Art Archive **67**; Erich Lessing/akg-images **18, 52, 74–75**; Musée du Louvre/akg-images **71a**; Alfredo Dagli Orti/Naval Museum, Genoa/The Art Archive **40**; Gianni Dagli Orti/Arquivo Nacional da Torre do Tombo, Lisbon/The Art Archive **60a**; Gianni Dagli Orti/Marine Museum, Lisbon/The Art Archive **27**; Gianni Dagli Orti/Museo Naval, Madrid/The Art Archive **80b**; Gianni Dagli Orti/National History Museum, Mexico City/The Art Archive **84**; Gianni Dagli Orti/Monastery of the Rabida, Palos/The Art Archive **36**; Gianni Dagli Orti/Museu Historico Nacional, Rio de Janeiro/The Art Archive **32b**; Gianni Dagli Orti/General Archive of the Indies, Seville/The Art Archive **51**; Gianni Dagli Orti/Royal Library, Stockholm/The Art Archive **65**; Kunstbibliothek, Staatliche Museen zu Berlin **96**; Courtesy Lilly Library, Indiana University, Bloomington **66, 77, 78–79**; Germanisches Nationalmuseum, Nuremberg/Bridgeman Art Library **13**; Bibliothèque nationale, Paris/Bridgeman Art Library **57**; The Stapleton Collection/Bridgeman Art Library **7**; From Bry, Theodore de *Das viendre Buch von der neuwen Welt*, 1613 **72**; Library and Archives, Canada **64**; *Head of Otegoongoon*. Engraving by Stanfield Parkinson, 1773. National Library of Australia, Canberra (nla.pic-an9308864) **109**; *Polus Antarcticus: Terra Australis Incognita*. Henricus Hondius, Amsterdam, 1642. National Library of Australia, Canberra (MAP T 727) **83**; *View of Huaheine*. Aquatint by Francis Jukes after a painting by John Cleveley. Published London, 1787. National Library of Australia, Canberra (nla.pic-an6016296); **2–3** *View of Matavai Bay*. Watercolour by John Cleveley, *c.* 1780. National Library of Australia, Canberra (nla.pic-an6503152) **106**; Newberry Library, Chicago **87**; Christie's Images Limited 2011 **177**; Statens Museum for Kunst, Copenhagen **20**; © Wolfgang Kaehler/Corbis **95**; From Codex Durán, Chap. LXXVII **92**; From Dati, Giuliano *Isole Trovate Nuovamente Per El Re di Spagna*, Florence, 1495 **47**; Biblioteca Medicea Laurenziana, Florence **97, 123**; Biblioteca Nazionale Centrale, Florence **86**; Joaquim Alves Gaspar, Wikimedia Commons **23l**; Museo Navale di Pegli, Genoa **39**; MS Hunter 242, Special Collections Department, Glasgow University Library **93**; Ethnographic Collection, Georg-August-Universität, Göttingen. Photo Harry Haase **82, 115**; Koninklijke Bibliotheek, The Hague (KB 78E fol. 48v) **63b**; From Hawkesworth, John *Account of the Voyages… in the Southern Hemisphere*, London, 1773 **105**; Caixa Geral de Depósitos, Lisbon; on loan to Museu Nacional de Arte Antiga, Lisbon/IMC **30–31**; Museu Etnográfico da Sociedade de Geografia de Lisboa, Lisbon **23r**; Museu de Marinha, Lisbon **25, 32a**; Museu Nacional de Arte Antiga, Lisbon **1, 19**; British Library Board **103** (Add. 21593C), **28** (shelfmark 10057.f.10); British Library, London **15, 24, 110**; British Museum, London **62, 63a, 122**; National Maritime Museum, Greenwich, London **16, 22, 100, 107**; The Natural History Museum, London **101, 114**; Royal Geographical Society, London **6**; The EbsKart project, University of Lüneberg **12**; Biblioteca Nacional, Madrid **85, 90**; Museo de América, Madrid **89b, 124**; Museo Naval, Madrid **58**; Mary Evans Picture Library **55, 61**; From Medina, Pedro de *Regimiento de navegación*, Seville, 1563 **21** (fol. 16), **49** (fol. 36); Museo Nacional de Historia, Castillo de Chapultepec, Mexico City **88**; Biblioteca Estense, Modena **14**; The National Archives, Kew **54**; Yale Center for British Art, Paul Mellon Collection, New Haven **71b**; Historic Maps Collection, Princeton University Library, New Jersey **80a**; Rare Books Division, Princeton University Library, New Jersey **17, 68**; Rare Books Division, The New York Public Library, Astor, Lenox and Tilden Foundations **37, 44**; The Pierpont Morgan Library, New York **33**; Germanisches Nationalmuseum, Nuremberg, MS 22414 **91**; Germanisches Nationalmuseum, Nuremberg, Hs 22474 **99** (on loan); John Nurminen Foundation **128**; Christ Church, Oxford. Courtesy of Pitt Rivers Museum, University of Oxford (1886.21.19) **108**; Bibliothèque nationale de France, Paris **8, 10, 35, 69, 76**; Academia de Bellas Artes de Puebla **98**; Courtesy of the John Carter Brown Library at Brown University, Rhode Island **73, 81**; Courtesy The Rooms Corporation of Newfoundland and Labrador, Provincial Museum Division **60b**; Biblioteca Casanatense, Rome, MS. 1889, ff. 96a-b, 97a-b **4–5**; Vatican Library, Rome **125a**; Courtesy National Museum of the Royal Navy, U.K. **118**; Museo Baluarte de Santiago, CONACULTA-INAH (Héctor Ceja) **94**; BPK, Bildagentur für Kunst, Kultur und Geschichte, Berlin/Scala, Florence **50**; Heritage-Images/Scala Florence **111**; The Newark Museum/Art Resource/Scala, Florence **42–43**; The Print Collector/Heritage-Images/Scala, Florence **9**; Biblioteca Columbina, Seville **38**; Museo de Bellas Artes, Seville **125b**; Dixon Library, State Library of New South Wales, Sydney **112, 113, 116**; Mitchell Library, State Library of New South Wales, Sydney **104**; National Palace Museum, Taipei **11l**; From Thevet, A. *Les singularites de la France Antarctique*, Paris, 1558 **41**; Mathieu Torck **11r**; Library of Congress, Washington, D.C. **48**; Jay I. Kislak Collection, Rare Book and Special Collections Division, Library of Congress, Washington, D.C. **45l, 45c, 45r**; Wellcome Library, London **70, 126, 127**; Photo Ken Wewerka **56**

Facsimile documents: Archivo de la Corona de Aragón, Ministerio de Cultura, España **2**; British Library Board (Add. 21593C) **8**; Journal of the H.M.S. Endeavour, 1768–1771. National Library of Australia, Canberra (Coll. no. MS 1) **7**; Biblioteca Nacional, Madrid **5**; The National Archives, Kew **3**; Rare Books Division, The New York Public Library, Astor, Lenox and Tilden Foundations **1**; David Rumsey Map Collection (www.davidrumsey.com) **9**; Jay I. Kislak Collection, Rare Book and Special Collections Division, Library of Congress, Washington, D.C. **6**; Beinecke Rare Book and Manuscript Library, Yale University, New Haven **4**

Index